NATURALLY DELICIOUS

Snacks & Treats

OVER 100 HEALTHY RECIPES

SQUIRREL
SISTERS

GRACIE AND SOPHIE TYRRELL

PAVILION

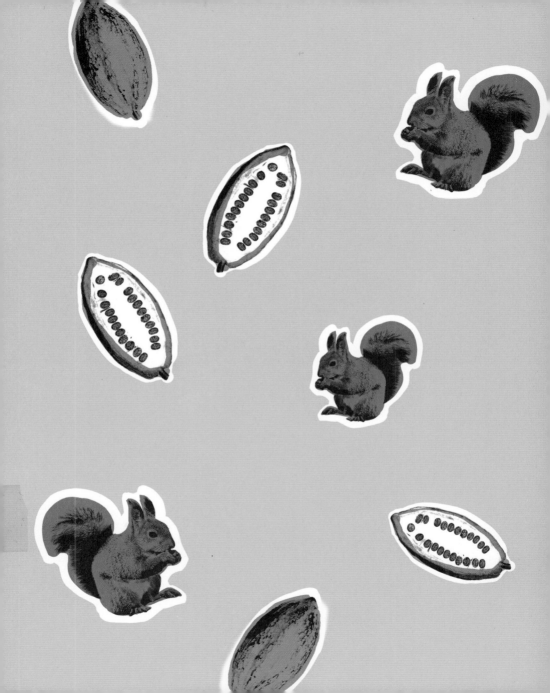

Hello!

Welcome to our Squirrel Sisters world, a world of delicious goodness that will satisfy your taste buds as well as your feed your health.

We are beyond excited to bring you our first ever cookbook; filled with our favourite recipes and a few from our family and friends. It's been a dream of ours to publish a recipe book so we are thrilled that it's now a reality and can share it with you in these pages.

We are Gracie and Sophie Tyrrell; sisters, besties and creators of Squirrel Sisters, a health and wellness company with a range of 100 per cent natural snack bars.

Our Squirrel Sisters story started in 2013 when we were both living on opposite sides of the world (Sophie in Singapore, Gracie in London). We are incredibly close; with similar interests and a minimal age gap (2 years and 1 week to be exact!) we were inevitably going to be inseparable. We pretty much do everything together and living on opposite sides of the world was a daunting thought, so we decided to start a blog because it was something fun to do together and it was a place to share all of our stories and discoveries. We've always had a passion for food, health and wellness; we've grown up with health conscious parents (our mum is a yoga teacher) who have always enjoyed good, healthy food. Food has always fascinated us – the effect it can have on our bodies, mind and mood is amazing!

We've always felt that there was a barrier that people often fought (and sometimes failed) to overcome when trying to live healthy lives and make healthy choices. 'Health' too often raises images of great effort and depriving yourself of the things you enjoy, and we want to change that.

We believe that eating healthily is all about balance; we are very normal girls, who love meeting up with friends for a glass of wine (or two) and overindulging in delicious eats at family get-togethers. All of our recipes and products are made with this in mind; we don't believe in restricting what you eat, we believe in fuelling your body with the right foods, that, when combined, together taste amazing!

We want to prove that being healthy doesn't have to be boring, that it can in fact be indulgent and delicious. That's why Squirrel Sisters was born... out of a love of food that made us feel great and most importantly tasted amazing! We decided to name it Squirrel Sisters because it was a nickname that has stuck with us since childhood ('squirrel' rhymes with our surname, Tyrrell).

As our blog grew we saw an opportunity to turn it into a business (something we had never originally set out to do). We launched our snack bars in November 2015 from the recipe Gracie created for Sophie when living together. Sophie has a gluten-intolerance, so the first bar was designed to give her an indulgent treat.

Our products are made using the highest quality whole ingredients; they are 100 per cent natural, raw, gluten-free, dairy-free, grain-free, have no added sugar and are suitable for people following a vegan and paleo lifestyle. It took a year to get everything sorted before we could launch our products; we had to find a factory that could replicate what we were making at home on a larger scale and then sort out the business side of everything. It's been a big job but we love it and wouldn't have it any other way. The best part about it is that we get to do it together!

Our love of cooking came from our mum who always made delicious meals when we were growing up (and still does... we always have the best meals when we go home for the weekend!) and some of her recipes have found their way into this book, too.

Our taste in food (other than for our bars) is actually quite different. We both like different things, which works well because it means we have always been very experimental with ingredients because one of us will always be able to taste test the other's recipes. And so the recipes in this book are a combination of things one or both of us love, some gluten-free, some dairy-free, and so on, but all delicious and designed to help you treat yourself.

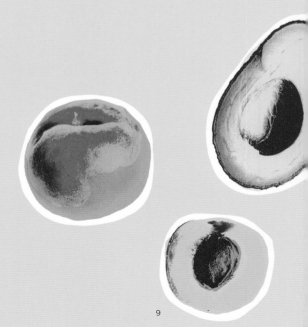

Squirrel Snacks and Treats

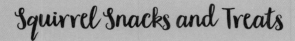
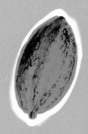

Our slogan is 'Treat Your Health', because we believe that you can have a treat (sweet or savoury) that can be good for you at the same time. Good-quality, well-made, healthy food does not need to be boring or tasteless – it can be delicious and indulgent, too!

In this book, we share 70 delicious recipes using ingredients that you can find in your local supermarket. All of our recipes are snack, share or 'on-the-go' sized because we want to make eating good food convenient and simple. They all use great ingredients, with health-properties and deliciousness to boot. The occasional recipe has something a little 'naughtier' because, let's be honest, a little bit of what you fancy does you good, too! It's all about balance.

Our recipes can be enjoyed at any time of day. A little piece of advice that we live by is to make things in advance, so you always have lots of goodies in the fridge or cupboard, ready to eat when the hunger pangs set in.

Breakfast is so important! It gives you the energy you need to tackle the day ahead. And yet, so many people seem to skip breakfast and the main reason for this is lack of time. So, in the Breakfast Time chapter we've included all of our favourite breakfast recipes that can be made in advance (often the night before), so you can grab and go in the morning... no more excuses for skipping your first meal of the day!

The On-the-Move chapter is for the busy bees out there. We have a selection of delicious recipes that are perfect for taking on-the-go so you never have to go hungry while out and about.

The best times are spent with others, laughing and making memories. There is no better occasion than sitting round a table with friends and family enjoying delicious food (and wine!). It's one of our favourite things to do, so of course we had to have a chapter on our favourite recipes to enjoy with others in Share the Love.

And last but not least, the Sweet Tooth chapter is for those that have a sweet tooth and like us LOVE treats. We can't express enough how much we believe in balance (we've mentioned it a few times already), so we have filled this chapter with some of our favourite sweet recipes, most of which have a nutritional twist. There are even a few cocktails to try!

Our top tip: preparation is key! Have the right ingredients in your fridge or pantry and prepare things in advance. We love spending our Sundays batch-cooking so we have lots of food prepared for the week ahead.

A NOTE ON INGREDIENTS

We want to make eating well as simple and convenient for you as possible, so, don't worry, we haven't included fairy dust and magical unicorns... just wholesome ingredients that you can find in your local store or supermarket.

Happy cooking, baking, freezing and blending! We really hope you love these snacks and treats as much as we do.

BREAKFAST TIME

Cocoa Porridge Bars (AKA chocolate flapjacks!)

Our take on a chocolate flapjack...
so good as well as nutritious!
Unsweetened pure cocoa powder
is packed with antioxidants, and
the cacao nibs give you that wake-
me-up hit to really get you going in
the morning!

Makes 12

150g/5½oz coconut oil
175g/6oz/⅔ cup runny honey
350g/12oz/2½ cups porridge oats
6 tbsp unsweetened cocoa powder
2 tbsp cacao nibs
a pinch of salt

Preheat the oven to 180°C/350°F/Gas
Mark 4, and grease and base-line a
25 x 20-cm/10 x 8-in baking pan with
baking paper.

Put the coconut oil in a small saucepan
and melt gently, then stir in the honey.

Combine all the remaining ingredients
in a large mixing bowl, and pour in
the melted oil and honey. Stir until
everything is well incorporated and all
the oats are evenly coated.

Tip the mixture into the prepared baking
pan and spread it evenly. Press it into
the pan so it's quite compact – a large
flat spatula or fish slice is useful for this.

Bake for 20 minutes until the top has
darkened in colour and it smells toasty.
Remove from the oven and allow to cool
in the pan and firm up (it will be very
crumbly when hot). Once cool, remove
from the baking pan and slice into
12 bars to serve or store.

Store in an airtight jar or container for
up to 1 week.

Vanilla Overnight Oats

...ts overnight makes them
...my and indulgent. Prep this
...akfast straight into the jars or
...rs you will be eating it from, so
...rab it and go in the morning.

...oz/scant 1¼ cups porridge oats
...3½fl oz/1¾ cups almond milk
½ tsp vanilla bean paste
2 tsp maple syrup
toppings of your choice, to serve (we
like fresh berries and chopped nuts)

Divide the oats evenly between
2 bowls, jars or containers. Add half
of the remaining ingredients to each
container and stir well. Cover with
clingfilm (plastic wrap) or the lids and
pop in the fridge overnight.

When you're ready to eat, sprinkle over
the topping of your choice and enjoy.

Mum's Granola to Go

We might be biased, but our mum's granola really is the best – she always has a fresh batch waiting for us when we return home. She created this bar version so that we never go without a hearty breakfast when we are busy.

Makes 12

200g/7oz/2 cups jumbo rolled (old-fashioned) oats
50g/1¾oz/½ cup roughly chopped pecans
50g/1¾oz/generous ½ cup flaked (sliced) almonds
25g/1oz/¼ cup goji berries
100g/3½oz/¾ cup mixed seeds
2 tsp ground cinnamon
100g/3½oz coconut oil, melted
150ml/5fl oz/⅔ cup maple syrup
a pinch of salt

Preheat the oven to 180°C/350°F/Gas Mark 4 and line a 20-cm/8-in brownie pan with baking paper.

Combine all the ingredients in a large mixing bowl and mix really well to combine.

Tip the mixture into the prepared pan and spread it evenly. Press down with a large flat spatula or fish slice to compress the mixture a little and make sure you have a nice, smooth top.

Pop the pan in the oven and bake for about 30 minutes, until golden on top. Check it halfway through, and if it looks like it is browning a little too quickly (or that the goji berries are going a bit dark), cover the top with a piece of foil.

Remove from the oven and let it cool in the pan for a few minutes and firm up. Use the baking paper to lift it out of the pan and onto a chopping board. Let it cool completely. Slice into 12 bars to serve or store.

Store in an airtight jar or container for up to 1 week.

Toasty Hazelnut and Cocoa Butter

A nutritional twist on a breakfast classic – who doesn't love hazelnut and chocolate spread?! We love eating it straight from the jar or spreading it over pancakes or toast. Depending on your food processor the timing can vary but trust us it's worth the wait once everything comes together.

Makes about 275g/9½oz

**250g/1¾oz/scant 2 cups hazelnuts
1½ tbsp unsweetened cocoa powder
1 tbsp granulated stevia (optional)**

Preheat the oven to 160°C/300°F/Gas Mark 3.

Tip the hazelnuts into a roasting pan and pop in the oven for about 10 minutes to toast them. Check them every 1–2 minutes after 5 minutes, as if they begin to darken too much they will add a bitter taste to the butter. You want them light golden.

Once cooked, tip them straight into the small bowl of a food processor and blend. You will need to blend for about 10–12 minutes in total, stopping every minute or so and using a spatula to scrape down the sides of the bowl. The nuts will go from a powder, to a rough paste, to a smooth butter as the oils get released. Once it's starting to look butter-like, add the cocoa powder and stevia, if using, and keep blending until the butter is as smooth as you can get it.

Store in an airtight jar or container in the fridge. It will keep for 1–2 weeks – if you can resist it for that long!

Sweet Roasted Almond and Cinnamon Butter

This nut butter doesn't last long in our houses... give this recipe a go and you'll understand why.

Makes about 250g/9oz

250g/9oz/2 cups whole almonds (with skins)
½–1 tsp pink Himalyan salt or sea salt flakes
1 tsp pure vanilla extract
2 tsp ground cinnamon

Preheat the oven the 180°C/350°F/Gas 4.

Tip the almonds into a roasting pan and roast for 8–10 minutes, until they have deepened in colour and are smelling lovely and toasty.

Allow them to cool for a couple of minutes, then tip them into a food processor and blend. You will need to blend for about 10 minutes in total, stopping every minute or so and using a spatula to scrape down the sides of the bowl. The nuts will go from a powder, to a rough paste, to a smooth butter as the oils get released. Once it's starting to look butter-like, add the salt, vanilla and cinnamon and keep blending until the butter is as smooth as you can get it.

Squirrel's Banana Bread

One of our first recipes on the blog, this new and improved version is just as delicious. Our friends love this banana bread so we're sure yours will, too.

Makes 1 loaf (10 slices)

50g/1¾oz coconut oil, plus extra for greasing
2 very ripe bananas
100g/3½oz/1 cup ground almonds
75g/2¾oz/⅔ cup buckwheat flour
½ tsp ground cinnamon
½ tsp ground ginger
1 tsp baking powder
75g/2¾oz sultanas (golden raisins)
60ml/2fl oz/¼ cup maple syrup
1 large (US extra-large) egg, lightly beaten
a pinch of ground pink Himalayan salt, or fine sea salt
a sprinkle of flaked (sliced) almonds

Preheat the oven to 180°C/350°F/Gas Mark 4 and grease and base line a 450g/1lb loaf pan with baking paper.

Put the coconut oil in a small saucepan and melt gently over a low heat.

Put the bananas in a bowl and mash with a potato masher until you have a chunky purée.

Combine the ground almonds, buckwheat flour, cinnamon, ginger, baking powder and sultanas in a large mixing bowl.

Once melted, add the coconut oil to the dry ingredients, along with the mashed banana, maple syrup, egg and salt. Mix with a wooden spoon until well combined, then pour into the prepared pan. Sprinkle the flaked almonds over the top of the batter.

Pop the loaf into the preheated oven and bake for about 30 minutes, or until golden on top and a skewer inserted into the centre of the loaf comes out clean. Check the loaf after 20 minutes and if it is browning too much in top, cover with a sheet of foil for the remaining cooking time.

Once cooked, allow to cool for 5 minutes in the pan, then turn out onto a wire rack and leave to cool completely, or slice and serve warm.

Breakfast Cups

Create cups from gluten-free wraps and fill them with all your breakfast favourites. **The crisp peaks of these breakfast cups were built for dipping – snap them off and dunk in the runny egg yolk.**

Serves 2–4 (depending on how hungry you are)

2 rectangular gluten-free wraps
a splash of olive oil
50g/1¾oz diced pancetta or chopped smoked bacon
80g/2¾oz mushrooms
1 large tomato, deseeded and diced
4 small eggs
freshly ground black pepper

Preheat the oven to 180°C/350°F/Gas Mark 4.

Cut the wraps in half diagonally into triangles. Fold each one into a hole of a jumbo muffin pan, so that the bottom is fully lined and the peaks stick upwards. (Warming them for a few seconds in the microwave may make them more pliable and easier to do this.) Cook the wraps in the preheated oven for 3 minutes to crisp up a bit, then set aside.

Heat the oil in a frying pan (skillet) set over high heat and fry the pancetta for a few minutes until it is crispy and golden. Remove it from the pan with a slotted spoon, leaving the fat in the pan. Add the mushrooms to the pan and fry until they are browned and softened, then add the tomatoes and warm through. Season with pepper (the pancetta will provide the salt). Divide the pancetta between the 4 bread cups, followed by the tomato and mushroom mixture. Crack an egg into each one.

Return the muffin pan to the oven and cook for 3 more minutes, then cover the cups with foil to stop the bread over-browning and cook for a further 10 minutes or so, until the egg white is opaque, but the yolk is still runny. Serve immediately.

Mini Vegan Mix-and-match Muffins

Who doesn't love a muffin for breakfast? You can decorate these beauties however you like and with whatever toppings you have in the cupboard. Even more, they are small enough to take with you on the go.

Makes 24

125g/4½oz grated apple (leave the skin on for more fibre)
50g/1¾oz coconut oil, melted
5 tbsp maple syrup
130ml/4½fl oz/½ cup almond milk
1 tsp pure vanilla extract
100g/3½oz/1 cup ground almonds
60g/2¼oz buckwheat flour
2 tsp baking powder
1½ tbsp chia seeds
1 tsp lucuma powder
a pinch of sea salt

TO TOP THE MUFFINS
dried fruit (goji berries, cherries, chopped apricots, raisins, etc.)
nuts, roughly chopped (hazelnuts, almonds, pistachios, walnuts, pecans, etc.)
seeds (sunflower, pumpkin, etc.)
cocoa nibs

Preheat the oven to 170°C/325°F/Gas Mark 3 and grease a 24-hole mini-muffin pan really well with coconut oil.

Get all your chosen toppings together before you start.

In a large mixing bowl, combine the grated apple, melted coconut oil, maple syrup, almond milk and vanilla, and stir together really well.

In another bowl combine all the remaining ingredients. Add half the dry ingredients to the batter and fold in, then fold in the remaining half.

Using teaspoons, spoon the batter evenly into the prepared muffin pan. Top the muffins with whatever fruit, nuts and other flavourings you wish.

Pop the pan in the oven and bake for 20–25 minutes, or until the muffins are risen, golden on top and cooked through. Check them after 15 minutes or so, and if they are browning too much, pop a sheet of foil over the top (sometimes the sugar in the dried fruit has a tendency to catch).

When baked, remove the pan from the oven and lay a clean kitchen towel over the top (the steam this creates will help unstick the muffins from the pan). After 5 minutes, either enjoy warm, or transfer to a wire rack to cool.

Coffee and Walnut Muffins

These muffins are gluten-free and packed with nuts for plenty of protein to help you feel full till lunchtime. Use barista-style fine coffee powder, not ground coffee, or your muffins will come out a little gritty!

Makes 6

100g/3½oz/1 cup ground almonds
150g/5½oz/generous 1 cup gluten-free plain (all-purpose) flour
100g/3½oz coconut palm sugar
1 tsp baking powder
1 tbsp fine instant coffee powder
a pinch of salt
100ml/3½fl oz/⅓ cup almond milk
50g/1¾oz coconut oil, melted
2 eggs, lightly beaten
100g/3½oz/⅔ cup walnuts, roughly chopped

Preheat the oven to 170°C/325°F/Gas Mark 3 and line a muffin pan with 6 large muffin cases.

Put the almonds, flour, sugar, baking powder, coffee powder and salt in a large mixing bowl and stir to combine. Add the almond milk, melted coconut oil and eggs, and beat everything together really well, then stir in the chopped walnuts, saving a small handful for the tops. (You can do all this in a stand mixer if you have one.)

Spoon the mixture evenly into the muffin cases and sprinkle the tops with the reserved walnuts. Pop in the oven and bake for about 20 minutes, until risen and with a crisp coat on top.

Remove from the oven and serve (these are delicious warm, fresh out the oven) or pack with you for breakfast on the go.

Mocha Breakfast Balls

A great grab-and-go breakfast snack that are even more delicious if you are able to heat them up in the microwave.

Makes 12

225g/8oz/1⅔ cups porridge oats
100g/3½oz mild, odourless coconut oil
(in a solid state, not melted)
2 tbsp fine instant coffee powder,
mixed with 1 tbsp water
4 tbsp granulated stevia
1 tsp pure vanilla extract
3 tbsp unsweetened cocoa powder,
plus extra for dusting

Put all the ingredients in a food processor and blitz to a rough paste.

Roll the paste into 12 balls, then roll the balls in extra cocoa powder to give them a light coating.

Eat 1 or 2 to give your day a kick start, and store the rest in the fridge for up to 4 days.

If you want to warm them up, simply blast for 10 seconds in the microwave.

Buckwheat Waffles with Coconut Cream

Really simple gluten-free waffles – you will need a waffle-maker to create these delicious breakfast treats. For a flavour variation, add 1 tsp of ground cinnamon to the batter and top them with a drizzle of Toasty Hazelnut and Cocoa Butter (see page 18) instead.

Serves 4

400-g/14-oz can coconut milk, put
   in the fridge overnight
120g/4oz buckwheat flour
1½ tsp baking powder
a pinch of salt
1 large (US extra-large) egg
200ml/7fl oz/generous ¾ cup milk
   of your choice
1 tsp pure vanilla extract
1 tbsp maple syrup, plus extra to serve
40g/1½oz coconut oil, melted and
   cooled a little

Start by making the coconut cream. Take the can of coconut milk out of the fridge and scoop the set cream off the top. Put it into a mixing bowl and beat with an electric hand whisk until light and fluffy. Pop it in the fridge until ready to serve.

Switch the waffle maker on to heat up to a medium heat. Heat the oven to low to keep the waffles warm when done.

Combine the buckwheat flour, baking powder and salt in a bowl.

In another bowl, beat the egg, then whisk in the milk, vanilla extract, maple syrup and coconut oil. Sift the dry ingredients into the bowl and whisk well to create a thick, lump-free batter.

Once the waffle maker has heated up, add one-quarter of the batter to the hot plate with a small ladle. Close the lid and cook for 2½ minutes, until risen and golden brown. Transfer the waffle to a baking dish covered in foil and keep warm in the oven while you cook the remaining 3 waffles in the same way.

Serve the waffles with the coconut cream and extra maple syrup for drizzling over the top.

Vegan Blueberry Pancakes

Pancakes made without any egg or dairy with a lovely crisp outer coating. Completely guilt-free, utterly delicious!

Serves 2 (makes 4)

1 tbsp chia seeds
120g/4oz/scant 1 cup gluten-free flour
1 tsp baking powder
a pinch of salt
100ml/3½fl oz/⅓ cup almond milk
½ tsp pure vanilla extract
a small handful of fresh blueberries
coconut oil, for frying
maple syrup or honey, to serve
   (optional)

Put the chia seeds in a small bowl and mix with 3 tbsp cold water. Leave to swell for a few minutes while you prepare the other ingredients.

Put the flour, baking powder and salt in a mixing bowl and make a well in the centre. Pour in the almond milk and whisk it in, being sure to get rid of any lumps of flour. Add the soaked chia seeds and vanilla, and whisk again until well incorporated. Stir in the blueberries.

Heat a little coconut oil in a non-stick frying pan (skillet) over medium heat. When hot, spoon in about one-quarter of the mixture and spread it out to a circle about 5mm/¼in thick. Cook for 2 minutes, until the underside is crisp and golden brown. Carefully flip over and cook the other side for another 1½–2 minutes until it is turning golden and the blueberries are lovely and jammy. Remove from the pan and keep warm while you cook the rest of the batter in the same way to make 4 pancakes.

Serve 2 pancakes per person with a drizzle of maple syrup or honey if you want a little extra sweetness (although the berries will provide a lot).

Pecan Pop Pancakes

We make these pancakes in batches in advance and freeze them so you can pop them in the toaster when you're ready to eat them. That way, you don't have to worry about eating them all in one go and have a reserve of perfect pancakes ready to whip out and toast on lazy days when you don't want to nip to the shops.

Serves 2–3 (makes 6)

200g/7oz/scant 1 cup cottage cheese
2 large (US extra-large) eggs
2 tsp vanilla bean paste
50g/1¾oz/⅓ cup porridge oats
60g/2¼oz pecans, roughly chopped
2 tbsp gluten-free flour
1 tsp baking powder
a pinch of salt
coconut oil, for frying
maple syrup, to serve

In a mixing bowl, beat together the cottage cheese and eggs to remove most of the lumps. Add the vanilla, oats, chopped pecans, flour, baking powder and salt, and beat again to mix everything together well.

Heat a little coconut oil in a non-stick frying pan (skillet) over medium heat. Once hot, pour a couple of spoonfuls into the pan and spread out to a circle about 10cm/4in wide and roughly 7mm/¼in thick. (If the pan is big enough to cook two at a time, go for it!) Cook the pancakes for 3 minutes, until golden and set underneath. Carefully flip over with a spatula and cook for another 2–3 minutes on the other side. Remove from the pan and serve immediately drizzled with maple syrup, or keep for another time.

If you are keeping the pancakes, let them cool completely on a plate. Place them in a strong freezer bag with a small piece of baking paper between each one. When you want to enjoy, simply remove them from the freezer and pop them straight in the toaster to reheat. Once out of the toaster, drizzle with a little maple syrup, and serve.

Baked French Toast with Apricot and Elderflower Compôte

A lighter version of French toast without butter. If you use gluten-free bread for this, like us, it takes longer to soak up the egg mixture than standard wheat bread. Therefore, soak your bread slices overnight to make sure they are not dry in the middle when you bake them.

Serves 2

2 large (US extra-large) eggs
80ml/2¾fl oz/5½ tbsp milk
2 tsp vanilla bean paste
2 thick slices gluten-free bread
coconut sugar, for sprinkling

FOR THE APRICOT AND ELDERFLOWER COMPÔTE
4 very ripe apricots, pitted and roughly chopped
2 tbsp good-quality elderflower cordial

The night before you want to have this for brekkie, whisk the eggs in a mixing bowl. Add the milk and vanilla, and stir in.

Put the slices of bread in a shallow dish and pour over the egg mixture. Turn the slices over in the liquid to make sure they are fully coated, then cover the dish in clingfilm (plastic wrap) and pop it in the fridge overnight.

The next morning, preheat the oven to 200°C/400°F/Gas Mark 6.

Using a fish slice or spatula, carefully transfer the bread slices to a baking sheet (they will be quite delicate). Sprinkle the tops of the slices with a little coconut sugar, and bake for 8–10 minutes, until the slices are golden brown and a little puffed up.

While the bread is baking, make the compôte. Put the chopped apricots in a small pan and sprinkle with a little water (you don't need much at all – just a few drops to stop the apricots sticking until they release their own juice). Pop a lid on the pan and place it over low heat.

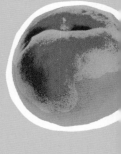

Cook gently for about 5 minutes, removing the lid and stirring every now and then, until the apricots have broken down to a chunky purée. Remove the pan from the heat and stir in the elderflower cordial.

Once the bread is baked and golden, transfer it to serving plates and top with the apricot compôte to serve.

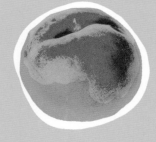

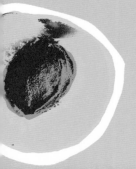

Healthy Hot Chocolate

We love hot chocolate! It's a classic comfort drink made even better with these nutritious ingredients that make you feel great.

Serves 2

500ml/17fl oz/2 cups almond milk
4 tbsp unsweetened cocoa powder
2 tbsp maple syrup
1 tsp pure vanilla extract

Put the milk in a saucepan and heat gently over medium heat until hot. Whisk in the cocoa powder, maple syrup and vanilla. Pour the hot chocolate into mugs, and enjoy.

FLAVOUR VARIATIONS

For a change, switch the vanilla for natural orange or peppermint extracts, or a tsp of ground cinnamon.

Chai Spiced Latte

A lovely spiced coffee to wake you up in the morning, with the added bonus of all the health properties from the spices. All the quantities below are suggestions and can be adjusted to suit your personal taste.

Serves 2

500ml/17fl oz/2 cups milk of your
    choice – whole (full-fat) milk is lovely,
    but substitute semi-skimmed or a
    dairy-free milk, if preferred
1–2 tsp chai spice blend (see page 136)
2–3 tsp fine instant coffee powder
2 tsp maple syrup

Simply put all the ingredients into a saucepan and heat gently until hot, but not boiling.

Pour through a tea strainer into mugs and enjoy.

Oat and Berry Breakfast Smoothie

A great smoothie to start your day! For those of you that like to press 'snooze' on your alarm, this can be made the night before so there's no thinking required in the morning.

Serves 2

250ml/8½fl oz/1 cup almond milk
30g/1 oz/4 tbsp porridge oats
160g/5½oz frozen mixed berries
1–2 tsp honey

Put all the ingredients in a blender, and blend until smooth.

Pour into 2 glasses or bottles with lids and serve whilst still very cold or store in the fridge until morning.

Piña Colada Breakfast Smoothie

This is a great way to use up any coconut water you have left over from making coconut cream, which we use in a lot of our recipes. Or, of course, you can use any carton of coconut water. Make sure you buy canned pineapple in juice and not syrup. Add a splash of rum and it doubles up as a deliciously creamy cocktail, although perhaps not for breakfast! Put all the ingredients in the fridge beforehand to chill to make it cool and refreshing.

Serves 2

400-g/14-oz can coconut milk, put in the fridge overnight
1 banana, peeled and frozen
227-g/8-oz can pineapple slices in fruit juice, put in the fridge overnight
2 tbsp desiccated (dried unsweetened shredded) coconut

Take the cold can of coconut milk out the fridge and open it up. Scoop out all of the solid cream from the top of the can. Tip the coconut water from the bottom of the can into a blender, then add in 2–3 tbsps of the coconut cream. Set the rest of the cream aside for whipping or using in another recipe.

Add the banana to the blender, along with the pineapple slices and all the juice from the can, and the desiccated coconut. Blend on full power until really smooth, light and fluffy.

Divide into 2 glasses and serve.

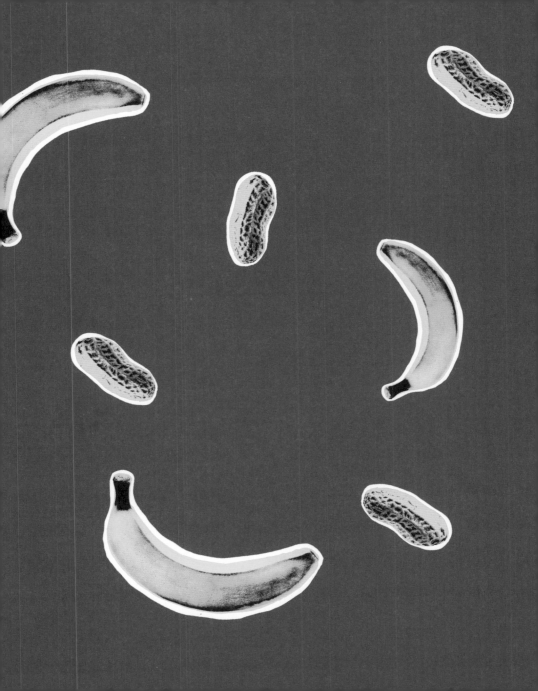

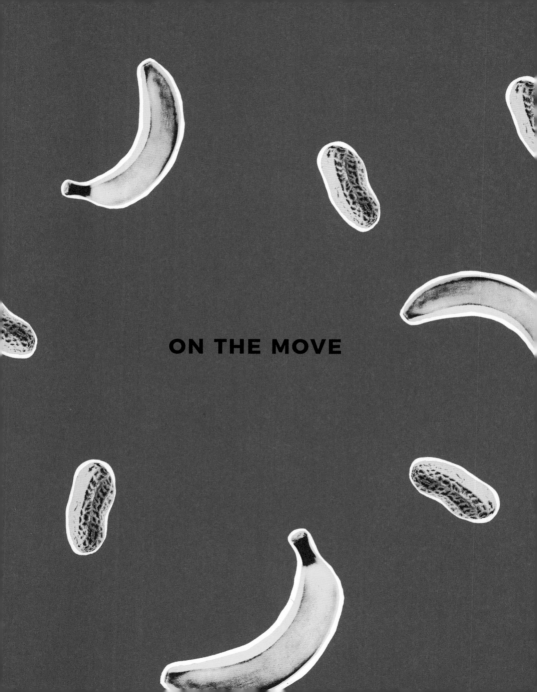

ON THE MOVE

No Ordinary Squirrel Sisters Bar

For those of you that love our bars, try making these de-constructed versions, perfect for squirrelling away to snack on throughout the day!

Makes as much as you want!

choice of snack-size treats from the ideas here, or make up your own!

No measurements needed, just use a handful of each ingredient from the suggestions here. Shake the ingredients together in an airtight container and take with you to enjoy.

CACAO BROWNIE

Cashew nuts, chopped dates, currents and organic cocoa nibs.

COCONUT CASHEW

Chopped dates, cashew nuts, coconut chips, sultanas (golden raisins), almonds and sunflower seeds.

CACAO ORANGE

Cashew nuts, chopped dates, currents, organic cocoa nibs and dried orange pieces.

RASPBERRY RIPPLE

Cashew nuts, chopped dates, sultanas (golden raisins), almonds, goji berries and freeze-dried raspberries.

Apple and Cinnamon Balls

These snack balls are so easy to make and use simple ingredients that everyone might have in their store cupboard. Apple and cinnamon is a winning combination and sweet enough to make the perfect afternoon pick-me-up!

Makes 12

200g/7oz/1¼ cups soft dates
50g/1¾oz/generous ½ cup dried apple
80g/2¾oz/generous ¾ cup ground almonds
2 tsp ground cinnamon

Put all the ingredients in a food processor and blitz to a rough paste.

Roll the paste into 12 balls and enjoy.

Store the balls in a cool dry place and keep them fresh in an airtight container.

Seed and Salted Honey Energy Balls

This recipe for snack balls is a great way to use up all those half-used packets of seeds that accumulate in the back of the cupboard (just like Mum's Granola To Go, see page 16). A sweet and savoury classic, which is perfect for when you're on the run.

Makes 12

300g/10½oz mixed seeds (pumpkin, sunflower, sesame, pine nuts, etc.)
20g/¾oz/1½ tbsp chia seeds
4 tbsp runny honey
1 tsp sea salt flakes

Preheat the oven to 180°C/350°F/Gas Mark 4. Tip the mixed seeds into a large roasting pan and roast for 6–7 minutes, stirring halfway through, until starting to turn golden.

Meanwhile, put the chia seeds in a small bowl with 1½ tbsp of water and leave them to swell up.

Once the mixed seeds are cooked, transfer them to a food processor and add the chia seeds and honey. Blitz until the mixture forms a coarse paste. You will need to stop the machine and scrape down the sides of the bowl with a spatula every 30 seconds or so to make sure they blend evenly. Once they are a paste and sticking together, quickly blitz in the salt flakes.

Tip the mixture from the food processor onto a plate and divide into 12 even portions. Form them into balls, then pop them in the fridge to chill until they have firmed up. Keep them in the fridge and enjoy when you need an energy boost.

Store the balls in a cool dry place and keep them fresh in an airtight container.

Lemony Za'atar Snacking Almonds

Za'atar is a Middle Eastern spice blend that is available in most supermarkets. It gives these spiced nuts a lovely tangy flavour. Get almonds with their skins still on as the wrinkles help to hold onto the flavourings, and the skins provide extra dietary fibre.

Serves 3–4

10g/⅓oz/2 tsp butter
2 tbsp lemon juice
100g/3½oz/¾ cup whole almonds
1½ tsp za'atar
½–1 tsp sea salt flakes

Preheat the oven the 180°C/350°F/Gas Mark 4.

Put the butter in an ovenproof frying pan (skillet) or a small baking pan and melt it gently over low heat. Add the lemon juice and almonds, and stir together so that the almonds are well coated in the juice and butter.

Transfer the pan to the oven and bake for 6–7 minutes, removing the pan from the oven every couple of minutes and giving it a good shake to stir everything around. Once done, the almonds should be a glisteningly golden brown and all the liquid in the pan should have gone.

Remove the almonds from the oven and, whilst still hot, sprinkle over the za'atar and salt flakes, starting with ½ tsp salt and adding more if wished. Allow to cool a little, so that they won't burn people's mouths, and serve warm.

Alternatively, allow to cool and divide into bags to take with you on the go.

Black Forest Trail Mix

Dark chocolate in bars is usually much better quality than the cooking chocolate drops, so buy a good high-cocoa-percentage bar and chop it yourself. The cocoa nibs really maximise the chocolate flavour, but can be a little bitter, so leave out if you're not a strong chocolate fan!

Serves 2

40g/1½oz dark (bittersweet) chocolate, at least 70% cocoa solids, roughly chopped
50g/1¾oz/⅓ cup dried cherries
50g/1¾oz/⅓ cup whole unblanched almonds
30g/1oz/⅙ cup unroasted buckwheat groats
10g/⅓oz/1 tbsp cocoa nibs (optional)

Mix all the ingredients together, then divide into bags to snack from.

Tropical Trail Mix

Our top tip with this recipe is to buy supermarket own-brand dried fruits. They tend to work better in this recipe as they are often softer.

Serves 2

20g/¾oz dried pineapple
15g/½oz/scant ¼ cup banana chips
20g/¾oz/½ cup coconut flakes
15g/½oz dried mango
20g/¾oz/2½ tbsp pumpkin seeds

Mix all the ingredients together, then divide into bags to snack from.

Topped Rice Cakes

There's no set recipe for this snack, it's just intended to inspire ideas for what to top your rice cakes with. You can also try any of the other pâté or houmous recipes from this book as a topping.

Makes as many as you need it to!

rice cakes
choice of toppings from the ideas here, or make up your own!

ENGLISH BREKKIE

Cook off slices of streaky (fatty) bacon until golden and crispy. Allow to cool, then crumble them (but not into dust!). Hard-boil (hard-cook) an egg and chop it. Add them to the bacon along with 1 small, diced, deseeded tomato and 2 tsp mayonnaise, and stir together. Season well with black pepper and a little salt (the bacon may provide enough salt), and pile onto rice cakes.

NUT BUTTER

Use either of the butter recipes in the book (pages 18 and 20), or buy organic sugar-free nut butters in the shops and spread them on.

CAJUN TUNA

Combine 1 small can of no-drain tuna, 1 tbsp mayonnaise, 1 finely sliced spring onion (scallion) and 1 tbsp cooked sweetcorn kernels in a bowl. Season well with salt and pepper and top the rice cakes. Finish with a sprinkling of Cajun spice blend on top.

GUACAMOLE

Add finely diced red chilli to the guacamole recipe on page 83 and pile it onto the rice cakes.

DELI READY

Raid the deli section of your local supermarket for semi-dried tomatoes, chargrilled artichoke hearts (and other Mediterranean veg), black olives and capers. Chop the tomatoes and other veg into very chunky pieces and combine with a little of the oil from the tomatoes, if needs be. Stir in the olives and capers and pile on top of rice cakes. Top with fresh basil, if you fancy.

Buttery Marmite Popcorn

Marmite, you either love it or you hate it and that's very true for the two of us – Sophie loves it, Gracie hates it! If you love it like Sophie, you can also add a cheesy dimension with a sprinkling of Parmesan or nutritional yeast flakes, if you're vegan.

Serves 2

a splash of olive oil
50g/1¾oz/¼ cup popcorn kernels
40g/3 tbsp salted butter
2–3 tsp Marmite (depending on how much you love it!)
1 tbsp finely grated Parmesan or nutritional yeast flakes (optional)

Put a splash of olive oil in a large saucepan with a lid. Add the popcorn kernels and pop the lid on. Heat over high heat until you begin to hear pops. Keep cooking, shaking the pan frequently so none stick and burn, until the popping subsides. Turn the heat off and leave it for another 30 seconds or so before removing the lid to make sure any late-popping kernels don't fly out at you.

While the popcorn cooks, put the butter and Marmite in a small saucepan and heat it gently to melt the butter – not forgetting about the popcorn as you do!

Once the corn is all popped and the butter melted, drizzle the Marmite butter over the popcorn, stirring gently all the time so that it is evenly distributed. Sprinkle over the Parmesan or yeast flakes, if using, and stir in. Tip into a serving bowl, discarding any un-popped kernels as you do, and serve.

Bacon Maple Popcorn

The ultimate sweet and savoury popcorn combo – you'll make this again and again!

Serves 2

2 slices dry-cure smoked streaky (fatty) bacon
a splash of olive oil
50g/1¾oz/¼ cup popcorn kernels
1 tbsp maple syrup
½ tsp sea salt flakes

Put the bacon in a non-stick frying pan (skillet) with a small splash of olive oil. Fry over high heat until crispy and golden all over, turning when needed so that it all browns evenly. Remove the bacon from the pan with tongs and leave to one side to cool.

Tip any fat left from the bacon into a large saucepan with a lid. Add the popcorn kernels and pop the lid on. Heat over high heat until you begin to hear pops. Keep cooking, shaking the pan frequently so that none stick and burn, until the popping subsides. Turn the heat off and leave it for another 30 seconds or so before removing the lid to make sure any late-popping kernels don't fly out at you. Tip the popcorn into a bowl, discarding any un-popped kernels.

Once the bacon has cooled and hardened a little, put it into a food processor and blitz to a coarse powder.

Drizzle the maple syrup over the popcorn, stirring gently all the time so that it is evenly distributed. Sprinkle in the bacon powder and sea salt flakes, mix well and serve.

Baba Ganoush

If you like Middle Eastern food you will love this dip. Don't be worried about putting the aubergine straight over the flame on the stove – you need a gas hob or a chef's blowtorch to create this one. It works better with 2 small aubergines rather than 1 large one as they are easier to cook through.

Serves 4–6

2 small aubergines (eggplants)
2 tbsp tahini
3 tbsp lemon juice
2 garlic cloves
1 tsp sea salt flakes
freshly ground black pepper

TO SERVE
a drizzle of olive oil
pomegranate seeds
fresh dill sprigs
crudités

Start by cooking the aubergines. Place each one directly over the flame on the stovetop. Cook for about 15–20 minutes, turning regularly with tongs to make sure all sides of the aubergines are charred. They will splutter and hiss from time to time, but that's fine – although you may need to give your stovetop a bit of a wipe down afterwards. Once they are softened all over and are smelling smoky, transfer them to a plate. Allow to cool for a few minutes until you can touch them without burning your fingers, then peel off and discard the skin and chop off the stalks. Roughly chop the aubergine flesh.

Put the aubergine into a food processor with the tahini, lemon juice, garlic and salt, and season well with black pepper. Use the pulse button to chop and combine the mixture, but make sure you keep a bit of texture in there. Adjust the seasoning to taste.

Transfer the baba ganoush to an airtight container and drizzle over a little olive oil. Scatter over some pomegranate seeds and small dill sprigs, and take with you for lunch. We take bags of crudités with us too, for dipping.

Homemade Spiced Tortilla Chips

If you want to really impress your friends then this recipe is great and super simple. For an extra kick, add some chilli flakes at the end with the sea salt.

Serves 2

2 gluten-free tortillas
2 tbsp olive oil
1 tsp sweet smoked paprika
½ tsp ground cumin
a sprinkling of sea salt flakes

Preheat the oven to 180°C/350°F/Gas Mark 4.

Using scissors, cut up the tortillas into rough triangles and lay them on a baking sheet.

In a small bowl, combine the olive oil, smoked paprika and cumin.

Use a pastry brush to brush the tops of all the triangles with the flavoured oil. Turn them all over and brush again on the other side to coat fully, then sprinkle them as liberally as you would like with sea salt flakes.

Pop the baking sheet in the oven and bake for 4 minutes. Remove from the oven and carefully turn all the chips over, then return to the oven for another 3–4 minutes until crisp and golden on both sides.

Allow to cool, bag up, then enjoy.

Sweet Potato, Caramelized Onion and Sumac Houmous

Sumac is a dried and powdered fruit that has an especially strong citrus flavour with a light kick of heat. With sweet potato and caramelised onion, this is delicate and sweet-tasting houmous – perfect with a selection of fresh crudités (such as celery, carrot and pepper sticks).

Serves 4–6

1 large sweet potato (about 400g/14oz)
5 tbsp extra-virgin olive oil, plus extra
    to serve
1 red onion, finely chopped
400-g/14-oz can chickpeas, drained
2 tbsp tahini
2 garlic cloves, roughly chopped
sea salt and freshly ground black
    pepper
a sprinkling of sumac

Put the sweet potato in the microwave and cook on high power for 8–10 minutes until soft and cooked through.

Meanwhile, heat 1 tbsp of the olive oil in a small frying pan (skillet) over low–medium heat and add the onion. Cook gently for about 10 minutes, until softened and light brown.

Scoop the cooked flesh out of the sweet potato skin and put it in a food processor. Add the chickpeas, tahini, garlic and the remaining olive oil, and blitz to a smooth purée. Season well with salt and pepper and pulse again to mix in. Add the cooked red onion and pulse a couple of times just to break the onion down slightly – it's nice to have a bit of texture in the houmous.

Scoop the houmous into an airtight container and top with a drizzle more olive oil and a sprinkling of sumac.

Beetroot and Caraway Crisps with Horseradish and Dill Dip

Super-healthy baked vegetables crisps with a Scandinavian twist served with a creamy and fiery horseradish and dill dip.

Serves 2

200g/7oz raw beetroot (beets) – about
    1 large or 2 small
1 tbsp olive oil
1 tsp caraway seeds
½ tsp sea salt flakes

FOR THE HORSERADISH AND DILL DIP
75g/2¾oz/⅓ cup light crème fraîche
½ tbsp creamed horseradish
a small handful of dill sprigs, roughly
    chopped
a squeeze of lemon juice
sea salt and freshly ground black
    pepper

Preheat the oven to 140°C/275°F/Gas Mark 1.

Peel the beetroot and, carefully and using the hand guard, slice it very thinly on a mandoline. You want each slice to be less than 1mm/¹⁄₁₆in thick.

Put the beetroot in a mixing bowl and toss with the oil and salt. Lay the slices out in a single layer over 2 non-stick baking sheets.

Bake for 20 minutes. Remove from the oven and turn the beetroot slices over using a pair of tongs. Return the baking sheets to the oven, switching them over so they cook evenly. Cook for another 15–20 minutes, until the beetroot slices are dried out.

Meanwhile, combine the crème fraîche, horseradish and chopped dill in a small bowl. Add a squeeze of lemon juice and season with salt and black pepper.

Once the beetroot slices are cooked, remove them from the oven and allow them to cool and crisp up a little more. Sprinkle them with salt and serve with the horseradish and dill dip.

Moroccan Harira Chickpeas

This snack is flavoursome, filling and perfect for picking at. The chickpeas are coated with ras-el-hanout, a classic Moroccan spice mix, and tangy lemon juice. Irresistibly good!

Serves 4

400-g/14-oz can chickepeas (garbanzo beans), drained and rinsed
2 tbsp olive oil
2 tbsp lemon juice
2–3 tsp ras-el-hanout spice mix (depending on how spicy you want them)
1 tsp flaked sea salt

Preheat the oven to 200°C/400°F/Gas Mark 6.

Put the chickepeas in a bowl and add all the remaining ingredients. Stir well to coat.

Tip the chickepeas into a roasting pan and spread out into an even layer. Make sure all the liquid goes in too, as the lemon juice will evaporate and leave a lovely tangy flavour on the chickepeas.

Pop in the preheated oven and roast for 10 minutes. Remove from the oven and stir everything around well, then return to the oven for another 10 minutes. Serve warm or allow to cool in the pan, then pack into small food bags in individual portions.

Roasted Provençal Chickpeas

All the flavours of your favourite pizza but coated around a crunchy chickpea... perfect for low calorie snacking. Make sure you dry the chickpeas really well with paper towels before cooking them so they go crispy in the oven.

Serves 2–4

400-g/14-oz can chickpeas (garbanzo beans)
1 heaped tbsp tomato purée (paste)
2 tbsp olive oil
2 tsp dried herbes de Provence
2 garlic cloves, crushed
1 tsp sea salt flakes
freshly ground black pepper

Preheat the oven to 200°C/400°F/Gas Mark 6.

Drain and rinse the chickpeas, then tip them onto a plate lined with paper towels, and leave to drain and dry.

Meanwhile, in a small bowl, combine the tomato purée, olive oil, dried herbs, garlic and salt, and season well with black pepper. Mix really well until the tomato purée is fully combined with the oil.

Tip the chickpeas into a large roasting pan and pour over the tomatoey coating. Stir really well to make sure that all the chickpeas are well coated. Spread out the chickpeas so that they are in a single layer and not all clumped together.

Bake them in the preheated oven for 20 minutes, stirring every 5 minutes or so, until golden and crisp on the outside. Serve warm or allow to cool and serve.

Sushi Rolls

Sushi makes a great healthy snack or lunch on the go. Fill them with plenty of fresh veggies and protein such as fish, cooked chicken, or tofu.

Serves 2

150g/5½oz/generous ¾ cup sushi rice
1½ tbsp rice vinegar
2 tsp honey
½ tsp salt
2 sheets sushi nori

FOR FILLING
tuna, drained
smoked salmon, sliced
prawns (shrimp)
cucumber, julienned
(bell) peppers, sliced
spring onions (scallions), julienned
carrots, julienned
avocado, sliced
mooli (daikon), julienned

TO SERVE
sushi ginger
wasabi paste
soy sauce

Start by preparing the rice so it can cool. Wash it well in a sieve (strainer) and leave it to drain. Put it in a small saucepan with 300ml/10fl oz/1¼ cups water and pop a lid on. Bring to a gentle simmer, then cook for about 10 minutes. Turn the heat off and leave it to sit for 10–15 minutes (without removing the pan lid), to finish cooking in the residual heat. Once cooked and tender, transfer the rice to a large plate and leave to cool.

Meanwhile, combine the rice vinegar, honey and salt in a small bowl. Stir together until the honey and salt have dissolved. Stir the seasoning into the cooled rice.

To make the sushi, place a sheet of nori onto a sushi rolling mat. Spread out enough rice to cover the sheet, leaving a 2-cm/¾-in border at the far end. On the side closest to you, create a line of whatever fillings you have chosen. Using the mat to help you, roll up the nori, trapping the fillings inside. Dampen the nori along the border, and finish rolling up so that the damp nori sticks to the roll, sealing it.

Slice the nori roll into about 5 smaller rolls with a very sharp knife and serve with sushi ginger, wasabi and soy, for dipping.

Sweet Potato and Thyme Croquettes with Paprika Ketchup

When we were little, we used to fight over the last croquette and we still do with these. They are amazing! The ketchup recipe will probably make more than you need, but you can freeze any leftovers as it makes a great quick pasta sauce.

Makes 12

2 large sweet potatoes (about 700g/25oz)
½ tsp ground cinnamon
2 tsp fresh thyme leaves
plain (all-purpose) or gluten-free flour, for dusting
2 eggs, beaten
50g/1¾oz/generous 1 cup panko or gluten-free breadcrumbs
vegetable oil, for frying
sea salt and freshly ground black pepper

FOR THE KETCHUP
1 red onion, finely diced
1 carrot, finely diced
2 tbsp olive oil
2 garlic cloves, crushed
400-g/14-oz can chopped tomatoes
1 tbsp sweet smoked paprika

Put the potatoes in the microwave and cook on high for 10–15 minutes, until they feel soft and cooked throughout. Allow them to cool.

Meanwhile, start the ketchup. Put the onion and carrot in a saucepan with the olive oil and cook gently over low–medium heat for about 8 minutes until the vegetables soften. Add the garlic and cook for another couple of minutes, then add the chopped tomatoes. Fill the tomato can about one-quarter full with water and swill it around, then tip the tomato water into the pan. Stir in the smoked paprika and cook for 20–30 minutes until thickened. Blitz with a stick blender until smooth, then season well.

Once the potatoes have cooled, slice them in half and scoop the flesh into a bowl, discarding the skins. Add the cinnamon and thyme leaves, and season with salt and pepper. Mix everything together really well until combined and there are no lumps of potato.

Put the flour in one shallow bowl, the beaten eggs in a second bowl and half of the breadcrumbs in a third.

Divide the potato mixture roughly into 12 and form the potato mixture into cylindrical croquette shapes. Dusting your hands with flour will help as the mixture may be quite sticky at this point. Roll the croquettes in flour, then in the egg, then in the breadcrumbs.

Once you have coated all the croquettes once, discard the breadcrumbs and tip the second half of the fresh breadcrumbs into the bowl. Coat the croquettes again, skipping the flour this time and just dipping them once again in the egg and then in the breadcrumbs so they all have a nice thick coating.

Heat the oil to 180°C/350°F and, once hot, add one-third of the croquettes to the pan. Fry them for about 3 minutes, until crispy and golden on the outside and hot throughout. Drain on a plate lined with paper towels and get the oil back up to temperature. Fry the second

batch, and then the third, in the same way and serve with the paprika ketchup for dipping.

Snack Frittatas with Greek Flavours

Pop these frittatas out of the pan and allow to cool completely, then bag one up to take with you for a filling snack, or with a salad for a light lunch.

Makes 6

100g/3½oz feta cheese, crumbled
40g/1½oz/generous ⅓ cup pitted (stoned) olives, sliced, whichever colour you wish
4 large (US extra-large) eggs
2 tbsp finely chopped Greek basil
½ tsp ground allspice
25g/1oz/scant ¼ cup pine nuts
freshly ground black pepper
olive oil, for greasing

Preheat the oven to 180°C/350°F/Gas Mark 4. Lightly grease the holes of a jumbo 6-cup silicone muffin mould and place it on a baking sheet.

Divide the crumbled feta and sliced olives evenly between the holes of the muffin mould.

In a mixing bowl, whisk the eggs really well, preferably with an electric mixer so they get really bubbly. Add the chopped Greek basil and allspice and whisk in. Season really well with black pepper (you won't need any salt as the feta and olives are both quite salty).

Divide the mixture evenly between the holes of the mould. You may need to add a little bit at a time to each, retuning once the bubbles have subsided to fit it all in, but this will make them lighter. Once all the egg mixture is in, sprinkle the pine nuts over the tops of the frittatas.

Pop the baking sheet in the oven and bake for about 15 minutes until golden on top and cooked through.

Lamb Koftas with Herby Tzatziki

Our koftas are great for all occasions and even more convenient because you can make a batch and freeze them. They are great on their own, in a salad or gluten-free wrap with a big dollop of tzatziki for creamy crunch.

Serves 4

2 tbsp olive oil
1 red onion, finely diced
3 garlic cloves, crushed
2 tsp ground cumin
2 tsp ground coriander
½ tsp ground cinnamon
½ tsp chilli flakes (hot red pepper flakes)
1 tsp sea salt flakes
500g/18oz lamb mince
1 large (US extra-large) egg
warmed flat breads, to serve

FOR THE TZATZIKI
125g/4oz/generous ½ cup Greek-style yogurt
120g/4oz chunk of cucumber, finely diced
1 tbsp olive oil
1 garlic clove, crushed
3 tbsp chopped mint
a good squeeze of lemon juice
sea salt and freshly ground black pepper

Start with the koftas. Put the oil in a large frying pan (skillet) and add the onion. Sauté it over gentle heat for a good 5 minutes until it is starting to really soften. Add the garlic, all the spices and salt, and cook for about 3 minutes more, until the garlic has mellowed a bit and the spices smell aromatic. Allow to cool for a few minutes.

Put the lamb mince in a bowl and add the onion and spice mix. Crack the egg in and stir everything together really well.

Divide the meat mixture into 8 and shape each portion into a long sausage shape around a small bamboo skewer. (The meat will be quite soft at this stage, but pop the skewers in the fridge, covered, for 20 minutes or so and they should firm up.)

Meanwhile, make the tzatziki. Combine all the ingredients in a bowl and season well with salt and pepper.

Once the koftas have chilled, drizzle a little oil over them and heat a non-stick griddle pan over medium heat.

Cook the koftas for 7–8 minutes, turning regularly, until brown all over and cooked through – you may need to do this in 2 batches, depending on the size of your griddle.

Serve the koftas on their skewers alongside the tzatziki and warmed flatbreads.

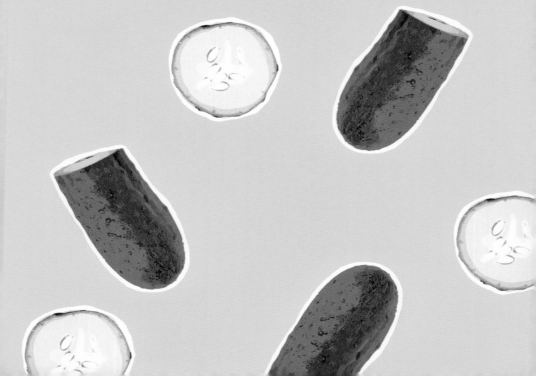

Chicken, Leek and Fennel Sausage Rolls

We make these 'no ordinary' sausage rolls with gluten-free puff pastry, but if you'd rather then use standard puff if you can for a slightly better rise. Both are delicious!

Makes 12

2 tbsp rapeseed oil
1 large leek, thinly sliced
1 large garlic clove, crushed
1 tsp fennel seeds
400g/14oz minced chicken
1 tsp sea salt flakes
½ tsp black pepper
1 pack ready-rolled puff pastry (Jus-Rol do a gluten-free version)
1 beaten egg, to glaze

Preheat the oven to 200°C/400°F/Gas Mark 6.

Heat the oil in a saucepan with a lid, over low heat, and add the leek, garlic and fennel seeds. Stir well to combine, then pop a lid on the pan and sweat down very gently for about 10–15 minutes, stirring from time to time so it doesn't catch on the bottom of the pan, until the leek is meltingly tender.

Meanwhile, put the minced chicken in a bowl and add the salt and pepper. Once the leek mixture is done, allow it to cool for a few minutes, then tip it into the chicken and mix everything together really well.

Lay out the pastry sheet on a lightly floured surface and cut it in half lengthways. Set one half aside. Spread half of the chicken mixture down the length of the first pastry strip, keeping it to the middle. Brush down one long side of the pastry with the beaten egg, then fold the other half over to meet it, enclosing the meat in the middle. Crimp the edge with a fork to seal, then, with a very sharp knife, cut the long sausage roll into 6 equal-sized smaller rolls. Move these to a non-stick baking sheet and repeat to make 6 more rolls with the remaining pastry and filling.

Brush all the rolls with beaten egg and pop the baking sheet in the oven.

Bake for about 18 minutes, until the pastry is puffed up and golden brown and the chicken is cooked through. Serve warm or cold – perfect for picnics!

Apple and Sage Scotch Eggs

These Scotch eggs have dried apple and sage in the sausage mixture – perfect partners for pork – to give them a lovely autumnal flavour. The meat layer on these needs to be reasonably thick because of the apple in there, or they may pop open when cooked.

Makes 6

6–8 quail's eggs (it's always good to have a few extras in case of accidents, so cook a couple more than you need!)
1 tbsp olive oil
1 small onion, finely diced
1 garlic clove, crushed
250g/9oz pork mince
6 large sage leaves, finely chopped
20g/¾oz/scant ¼ cup dried apple, finely diced
plain (all-purpose) or gluten-free flour, for dusting
60g/2oz/1⅓ cup panko or gluten-free breadcrumbs
2 eggs, lightly beaten
vegetable oil, for frying
sea salt and freshly ground black pepper

Cook the quail's eggs in boiling water for 2 minutes. Remove from the heat and run them under cold water until cool.

Very carefully peel off the shells. Set aside. Heat the oil in a small frying pan (skillet) over low–medium heat. Add the onion, and cook gently for about 5 minutes until beginning to soften. Add the garlic, and cook for another few minutes until the garlic and onion are both cooked and beginning to caramelize. Turn off the heat and leave to cool a little.

Put the pork mince in a mixing bowl and add the onion mixture, chopped sage and dried apple. Season well and mix everything together.

Divide the mixture into 6 rough portions. Take the first portion and flatten it into a thick-ish patty in the palm of your hand. Place a peeled quail's egg in the centre and wrap the meat around the egg very gently – the egg should be soft-boiled (soft-cooked), so will break easily. Smooth the meat into a neat ball and repeat with the other eggs and patties.

Now set up a production line. Put the flour in one shallow bowl, the beaten eggs in a second bowl and the breadcrumbs in a third bowl. Dip the eggs first in the flour to coat, then in the egg, and finally in the crumbs. Once all the eggs are coated, double coat them in the egg and breadcrumbs.

Fill a deep saucepan about one-third of the way up with vegetable oil and heat it over a medium heat to about 175°C/350°F (a few breadcrumbs should sizzle and bubble a little when thrown into the oil).

Cook the eggs, a couple at a time, for about 4½ minutes, until golden and crisp on the outside and the meat is cooked all the way through. Drain on paper towels before serving warm or cool completely and pack for lunch.

Chicken Tagine Parcels

All the flavours of a Moroccan feast, wrapped up in a handy parcel to go.

Makes 6

1 tbsp olive oil
1 onion, finely diced
2 garlic cloves, finely chopped
2 tsp ras-el-hanout spice blend
1 small preserved lemon, rind finely
    diced and flesh discarded
250g/9oz cooked chicken, shredded
50g/1¾oz/⅓ cup dried apricots,
    chopped
50g/1¾oz/½ cup pitted (stoned) green
    olives, sliced
25g/1oz flat-leaf parsley
6 large sheets filo (phyllo) pastry
    (roughly 48 x 24cm/19 x 9½in)
75g/2¾oz/5 tbsp butter, melted

Preheat the oven to 180°C/350°F/Gas Mark 4 and lightly grease a large baking sheet.

Heat the oil in a large frying pan (skillet) over medium heat and add the onion. Cook for about 5 minutes until beginning to soften. Add the garlic, ras-el-hanout and preserved lemon and continue to cook for a few more minutes until the onion is completely soft and translucent. Stir in the shredded chicken, apricots and olives, and cook for a couple of minutes to warm everything through.

Rip the top two-thirds off the parsley bunch, discarding the bottom stalks (it doesn't matter if some stalks go in as they add a bit of flavour). Chop the herb roughly then stir into the mixture. Taste and season with salt and pepper – you probably won't need too much salt as the preserved lemon is quite salty. Set aside.

Take the first sheet of filo and cut it in half to make 2 squares. Keep the rest wrapped in clingfilm (plastic wrap) so that it doesn't dry out and become brittle. Brush one square with the melted butter and place the other one on top. Spoon one-sixth of the chicken filling into the middle of the filo square and gather up all the pastry edges around it. Pinch them in the middle to seal them like a moneybag with a gathering of pastry at the top. Brush the whole outside of the pastry with melted butter and gently move it to the prepared baking sheet. Repeat with the remaining filo sheets and filling to make 6 parcels.

Cut 6 squares of foil and use them to make little hats for the filo, gathered at the top of the parcels. This will brown much quicker than the other bits of the parcel, so it's best to cover them at first, then brown them for the last few minutes of cooking. Carefully pinch the foil squares around the top of the parcel, stopping at the bottom of the neck and being carefully not to squash the nice pastry ruffles flat.

Pop the baking sheet in the oven and bake the parcels for about 25 minutes, until they are golden brown. Remove the foil tops for the last 5 minutes of cooking so that the tops can brown to the same shade as the rest of the parcels. Enjoy warm or cold.

Sun-dried Tomato and Herb Falafel

These may not be the most beautiful snacks on the outside but it's what's on the inside that really counts. Enjoy them in a wrap, with a fresh salad or pair them with one of our dips such as the Herby Tzatziki (see page 68) or Baba Ganoush (see page 54).

Serves 4 (makes 12)

1 onion, finely diced
2 tbsp olive oil
3 large garlic cloves
1½ tsp ground cumin
1½ tsp ground coriander
2 tsp sea salt flakes
400-g/14-oz can chickpeas (garbanzo beans), drained
4 tbsp gram flour
15g/½oz fresh coriander (cilantro), leaves and stalks, roughly chopped
15g/½oz flat-leaf parsley, leaves and stalks, roughly chopped
100g/3½oz sun-dried tomatoes, chopped into chunky pieces
vegetable oil, for frying
freshly ground black pepper

In a frying pan (skillet) set over medium heat, fry the onion in the oil for about 5 minutes until really beginning to soften. Add the garlic, spices and salt, and fry for a few minutes more until the onion is soft and translucent.

Tip the onion mixture into a food processor and add the chickpeas and gram flour. Blend until you have a coarse paste, which clumps together when squeezed. Quickly pulse in the herbs (you want to see clear flecks in the mixture), then remove the blade and stir in the chopped sun-dried tomatoes. Season with black pepper, and a little more salt, if you think it needs it.

Divide the mixture into 12 portions and roll each one into a ball. Place on a work surface and press down a little to make small patties about 1.5cm/½in thick.

Fill a non-stick frying pan (skillet) to a depth of about 5mm/¼in with vegetable oil and heat it over medium heat. Once hot, add the falafels to the pan and fry them for about 3 minutes on each side until golden brown (you may need to do this in 2 batches, depending on the size of your pan). Remove from the pan with a slotted spoon and drain on paper towels before eating.

SHARE THE LOVE

Pecorino and Almond Crisps with Fresh Figs

Pecorino is a strong salty cheese, which is the perfect match for sweet, sticky figs. Use fresh Pecorino so it melts properly and sticks together. These take minutes to make and look gorgeous (so instagramable!)

Makes 12

**100g/3½oz Pecorino cheese
30g/1oz/⅓ cup ground almonds
1 tsp dried thyme
freshly ground black pepper
finely sliced fresh figs, to serve**

Preheat the oven to 180°C/350°F/ Gas Mark 4 and line 2 baking sheets with non-stick baking paper or silicone sheets.

Finely grate the Pecorino and put it in a mixing bowl. Add the ground almonds and thyme, season with black pepper and mix everything together well.

Place a 9-cm/3½-in round cookie cutter on one of the prepared baking sheets, sprinkle in a small handful of the cheese mixture and spread out evenly with your fingertips. Carefully remove the ring and repeat to make 12 rounds in total, 6 on each sheet.

Pop the sheets in the oven for 8 minutes, until the cheese has melted, melding everything together, and turned lightly golden – you may need to swap the sheets over onto alternate shelves after about 5 minutes. Remove from the oven and allow to cool completely and firm up on the baking sheets.

Top each one with a thin slice of fresh fig and enjoy!

Five-spice Cavolo Nero Crisps

So easy and so delicious! These spiced vegetable crisps are the perfect lunchtime snack, or dinner-party treat. Make sure you don't overcook them as they will taste bitter if burnt!

Serves 2

100g/3½oz cavolo nero
1 tbsp sesame oil
1 tbsp rapeseed oil
2 tsp Chinese five-spice powder
sea salt

Preheat the oven to 140°C/275°F/Gas Mark 1.

Strip the cavolo nero leaves from the thick stalk and tear it into large pieces. Put them in a large bowl.

In a separate small bowl, combine the oils and five-spice, and stir together well. Tip the mixture over the leaves and mix until the leaves are thoroughly coated all over. Lay them out in a single layer on a baking sheet.

Put the cavolo nero in the preheated oven for 15 minutes, then remove the baking sheet and carefully turn them all over. Cook for another 5 minutes or so to finish drying them out. By this time they should be crisp and darkened slightly, but still green.

Remove the cavolo nero from the oven and allow to cool. Sprinkle with sea salt to serve.

Roasted Red Pepper, Rosemary and Cashew Pâté

A delicious creamy and filling vegan pâté that's packed with plant-based protein. Soaking the cashews overnight activates all the health-giving properties of the nuts. Serve with crudités, chips or crackers – whatever takes your fancy!

Serves 2

100g/3½oz/generous ¾ cup unsalted cashews
2 red (bell) peppers
1½ tbsp olive oil
1 heaped tsp chopped fresh rosemary needles
¼ tsp sea salt flakes
a splash of lemon juice
sea salt and freshly ground black pepper

Put the cashew nuts in a bowl and cover with cold water. Cover the bowl with a plate and leave to soak overnight.

The next day, preheat the oven to 180°C/350°F/Gas Mark 4. Slice the peppers in half lengthways and remove the seeds. Place in a small roasting pan and drizzle over ½ tbsp of the olive oil. Roast for 20 minutes until the peppers are softened and the skins are beginning to blacken and blister. Remove the peppers immediately to a small bowl, cover with a piece of clingfilm (plastic wrap) and leave to cool for 10 minutes – trapping in the steam in this way will help to remove the skins from the peppers.

Meanwhile, drain the cashews and put them in a food processor. Add the rosemary and salt, and blend until broken down into small pieces.

Returning to the peppers, peel off and discard the skins. Put the peppers in the food processor with the cashews, also adding any juices that have accumulated at the bottom of the bowl. Add the remaining 1 tbsp olive oil and blend until smooth and creamy. Season with a little more salt, if you think it needs it, plenty of black pepper, and a splash of lemon juice to lift the flavour.

Chunky Guacamole

Homemade guacamole is the best! Use it as a dip, to top rice cakes (see page 50), in a sandwich or salad... or just eat with a fork straight from the bowl.

Serves 2

1 avocado, roughly diced
1 large tomato, deseeded and diced
zest of 1 lime and juice of ½
1 spring onion (scallion), very finely sliced
1 tbsp finely chopped coriander (cilantro) leaves
sea salt flakes and freshly ground black pepper

Put the avocado in a small mixing bowl and mash with a fork until it starts to break down and any really large lumps are removed. Keep plenty of texture so it stays quite chunky.

Add all of the remaining ingredients and mix well to combine. Season well with salt and pepper and serve.

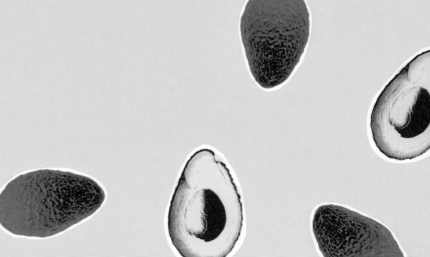

Texan Tato Tornados

The cutting of the potatoes is a bit tricky to start with, but once you've cracked that, nothing else could be simpler. The spice rub makes plenty, so sprinkle on as much as you like (be careful, it's quite spicy!) and keep the rest in a sealed jar for next time.

Serves as many as you want!

1–2 waxy potatoes per person
olive oil, for drizzling
sea salt flakes
BBQ sauce, to serve

FOR THE TEXAN SPICE RUB
2 tsp dried oregano
2 tsp garlic salt
2 tsp mild chilli powder
1 tsp ground cumin
½ tsp mustard powder
1 tsp cayenne pepper
2 tsp sweet smoked paprika
½ tsp ground black pepper

Preheat the oven to 190°C/375°F/Gas Mark 5.

Combine all of the spice rub ingredients in a small bowl and set aside.

Insert a metal skewer into a potato so that it runs down the entire length of the potato. Place the potato on a chopping board and position a small, sharp knife at the far right-hand side of the potato at a slight angle with the knife tip pointing to the right. Slice down until the knife hits the skewer and then begin to turn the potato so the knife works it's way down the length of the potato, keeping the knife at a slight angle so that you are slicing the potato with just 1 continuous cut. Once the knife has got all the way through the potato, you should be able to spread the slice to create a spiral on the skewer.

Cut as many potatoes as you need to and put them on a baking sheet. Drizzle with oil and sprinkle with the spice mix. Cook for about 30 minutes, turning them over occasionally and brushing with the spicy oil that will have accumulated on the sheet. Once they are golden and crisp all over, sprinkle with salt and serve with BBQ sauce for dipping.

Smoked Paprika Sweet Potato Fries

Sweet potatoes don't go crisp like standard ones, so sprinkling them with polenta on the outside helps to give them crunch – it's even better if you add a little sweet paprika to it!

Serves 2

1 large sweet potato (about 400g/ 14 oz)
25g/1oz/⅙ cup quick-cook polenta (cornmeal)
½ tsp sweet smoked paprika
1 tsp sea salt flakes
a drizzle of olive oil

Preheat the oven to 180°C/350°F/Gas Mark 4.

Cut the sweet potato lengthways into long fries. Put them into a steamer set over a pan of boiling water and steam for 5–6 minutes until beginning to soften (doing this will also help the polenta stick to the fries.)

Meanwhile, combine the polenta, paprika and salt in a small bowl.

Once softened, transfer the fries to a large baking sheet or two and drizzle with the olive oil. Stir gently to coat well, then sprinkle over the polenta mixture so that the fries are evenly coated. Pop them in the oven and cook for 10 minutes, then give them a stir around. Return to the oven for another 10–15 minutes, until they are crisp and golden. Serve hot.

Avocado Fries with Cool Chipotle Dip

Cooked avocado, served hot, may sound a little out there but, trust us, it is delicious. These fries are crisp on the outside and soft and creamy on the inside. Make sure your dip is fresh from the fridge and really cold as it makes for a taste explosion – spicy hot fries with cold, crisp and creamy dip, so yummy!

Serves 2

1 large avocado
plain (all-purpose) or gluten-free flour, for dusting
1 large (US extra-large) egg, beaten
30g/1oz/⅔ cup panko or gluten-free breadcrumbs
sea salt and freshly ground black pepper

FOR THE CHIPOTLE DIP
3 tbsp light crème fraîche
1 tsp smoked chilli paste

Preheat the oven to 180°C/350°F/Gas Mark 4 and lightly grease a baking sheet.

Slice the avocado in half and remove the stone (pit). Peel off the skin and slice each half into 6 wedges.

Put the flour in a shallow bowl and season it well with salt and pepper. Put the beaten egg in a second bowl and the breadcrumbs in a third.

Dip each avocado slice first in the flour, to dust it lightly, then in the beaten egg, then cover really well with the breadcrumbs and place on the baking sheet. Place the sheet in the oven and bake for 15–18 minutes, turning over halfway through, until golden and crispy.

While the avocado is baking, make the dip. Simply combine the crème fraîche and chilli paste and put in the fridge to stay cold until the avocado is ready, then serve together.

Stuffed Avocado with Chicken, Tarragon and Lime

This is a great way to get rid of any leftover cooked chicken from the Sunday roast. You can swap the crème fraîche for yogurt or a dairy-free alternative if you prefer. Perfect as a mid-morning snack or light lunch.

Serves 1–2

100g/3½oz cold cooked chicken, shredded
zest and juice of ½ lime
1 tbsp chopped tarragon
1 heaped tbsp crème fraîche (low-fat, if so wished)
1 avocado
sea salt and freshly ground black pepper

Put the chicken in a bowl and add the lime zest, tarragon and crème fraîche. Season well with salt and pepper and mix everything together well.

Slice the avocado in half and remove the stone (pit). Rub the cut side of the avocado with the lime juice to stop the flesh from browning. Pile half the filling into the hole in each avocado and serve with spoons to scoop the avocado and filling out of the skin.

Baked Cauliflower Pakoras

These baked cauliflower pakoras have a crisp, golden, spiced crust without the usual grease of a traditional pakora. This recipe works best with a romanesco cauliflower, but you can use a normal cauliflower, too. They are delicious served with the Coriander and Garlic Raita on page 94, or with a chutney of your choice.

Serves 4

1 romanesco or standard cauliflower, cut into florets
100g/3½oz gram flour
1 tbsp garam masala
1 tsp ground turmeric
1 tsp chilli powder
½ tsp garlic salt
½ tsp fine sea salt
130ml/4½fl oz/½ cup almond milk
2 tbsp rapeseed oil
sea salt flakes
Coriander and Garlic Raita (see page 94) or chutney of your choice, to serve

Preheat the oven to 200°C/400°F/Gas Mark 6 and line a baking sheet with baking paper.

Put the cauliflower florets in a large pan of boiling salted water. Once the water has returned to the boil, blanch them for 3 minutes until beginning to soften. Drain them in a colander and set aside while you make the batter.

Sift the gram flour into a large mixing bowl and add the spices and salts. Stir in the almond milk and oil until you have a smooth batter.

A few at time, drop the florets into the batter and coat them fully. Let the excess run off (the batter is quite thick so they should have a nice coating) and place on the prepared baking sheet.

Put the baking sheet in the oven and bake for about 25 minutes, or until the batter is golden and crunchy. Sprinkle with salt flakes and serve hot with raita or the chutney of your choice.

Charred Padrón Peppers

These are so quick to prepare and a little different from the usual party snacks and nibbles. They are also one of your five-a-day!

Serves 2

1 tbsp olive oil
160g/5¾oz Padrón peppers
a good pinch of sea salt flakes

Heat the oil in a large frying pan (skillet) or wok over medium–high heat. Add the peppers, and toss and stir-fry them for about 3 minutes, until they really start to soften, and the skins darken and blister (but don't burn them!).

Add the salt to the pan and toss so that they are well coated, then transfer to a serving dish and serve immediately.

Garlic Prawns with Tarragon Mayo

Making mayo is actually a lot easier than you expect, it just requires a little patience. The prawns and mayo go so well together that it's worth making for friends.

Serves 4

plain (all-purpose) or gluten-free flour, for dusting
2 eggs, beaten
60g/2oz/1⅓ cup panko or gluten-free breadcrumbs
2 tsp garlic salt
360g/12½oz raw king prawns (jumbo shrimp)
vegetable oil, for frying

FOR THE TARRAGON MAYO
1 egg yolk
½ tsp Dijon mustard
150ml/5fl oz/⅔ cup mild and light olive oil
2 tbsp lemon juice
finey grated zest of 1 lemon
20g/¾oz tarragon, leaves stripped from stalks and roughly chopped
sea salt and freshly ground black pepper

Start by making the tarragon mayo. Put the egg yolk in a bowl and stir in the mustard. Add the tiniest bit of olive oil and whisk in. Once incorporated, add another few drops of oil and whisk in again. Do this until the mixture starts to emulsify, then you can start adding the oil a little more quickly. (If you add it too quickly too early, the mixture may curdle.) Keep whisking and adding oil a little at a time until all the oil is added. If the mixture is getting a bit too thick for you to whisk, add the lemon juice to loosen it. Stir in the lemon zest and chopped tarragon, and season.

To prepare the prawns, put the flour on a plate and the beaten egg in a shallow bowl. In another shallow bowl, combine the breadcrumbs and the garlic salt. Dip each prawn first in the flour to lightly coat, then in the beaten egg, and finally in the garlicky crumbs.

Put the vegetable oil in a saucepan and heat to about 170°C/325°F. Fry the prawns, a few at a time, for about 1½ minutes, until golden on the outside and cooked through. Remove from the oil and drain on paper towels. Serve hot with the tarragon mayo for dipping.

Squirrels' Fish Fingers

A healthy twist on the classic fish and chips, which is a huge hit with our family – even those who are loyal to the local chippy!

Serves 2

70g/2½oz/⅔ cup ground almonds
finely grated zest of ½ lemon
1 garlic clove, crushed
½ tsp paprika
¼ tsp cayenne pepper
¼ tsp sea salt flakes
300g/10½oz white fish, such as cod or haddock
1 small egg, beaten
lemon wedges, to serve (you can use the lemon you have zested)

Preheat the oven to 180°C/350°F/Gas Mark 4 and lightly grease a baking sheet.

In a shallow bowl, combine the ground almonds, lemon zest, crushed garlic, paprika, cayenne and salt flakes. Rub everything together with your fingertips so that the garlic and lemon zest aren't clumped together.

Cut the fish into 6–8 chunky fingers.

Set up your production line, putting the beaten egg into another shallow bowl and having your baking sheet ready. Dip the fish fingers into the egg and turn to fully coat, cover them in the breadcrumbs, then place them on the baking sheet.

Pop the baking sheet in the oven and bake for 10–12 minutes, or until the coats are crisp and the fish is just cooked and opaque throughout.

Serve with lemon wedges for squeezing.

Salmon Skewers with Lemony Rocket Pesto

Lovely, zesty pesto goes really well with fish so long as you leave out the usual Parmesan. Try to buy the slimmer in width, but thicker in general fillets of salmon so you can get 5–6 chunky dice out of each one. Thinner fillets won't hold onto the skewers quite so well.

Serves 2

2 chunky salmon fillets (about
   360g/12½oz)
8–12 cherry tomatoes
olive oil, for frying

FOR THE PESTO
40g/1½oz rocket (arugula)
15g/½oz/⅛ cup pine nuts
zest of 1 small lemon
1 tbsp lemon juice
1 tsp sea salt flakes
3 tbsp extra-virgin olive oil
freshly ground black pepper

Start by making the pesto. Put the rocket, pine nuts, lemon zest and juice, sea salt flakes and olive oil in a food processor and blend until smooth. Season with black pepper and a little more salt, if wished, to taste.

Chop the salmon into 2.5–3-cm/ 1–1¼-in chunks and pop them in a bowl. Add half of the pesto and stir to coat the salmon well. You can leave this to marinate in the fridge if you have time, or just cook them straight away.

Thread the salmon chunks onto short skewers, alternating with the cherry tomatoes. You should get 4–6 skewers in total.

Heat a splash of olive oil in a large non-stick frying pan (skillet). Add the skewers and cook for about 10 minutes in total, turning every couple of minutes so that each of the sides gets browned.

Serve with the remaining pesto drizzled over the top.

Chicken Tikka Skewers with Coriander and Garlic Raita

Cook these chicken tikka skewers in a large frying pan or on a barbecue grill. Pile into warmed flatbreads (we use gluten-free!) and spoon the raita over the top – delicious!

Makes 6

2 large chicken breasts
1 tbsp olive oil, plus extra for frying
1 tsp ground cumin
1 tsp ground coriander
1 tsp paprika
1 tsp mild curry powder
½ tsp turmeric
½ tsp garam masala
½ tsp sea salt flakes
flatbreads, to serve (optional)

FOR THE RAITA
200g/7oz/1 cup thick natural (plain) yogurt
2 garlic cloves, crushed
25g/1oz fresh coriander (cilantro), finely chopped
½ tsp salt flakes
a squeeze of lemon juice

Chop the chicken breast into chunky dice, about 2.5-3-cm/1-1¼-in square.

Mix all the remaining skewer ingredients together in a small bowl and add the chicken. Mix around really well so that the chicken is fully coated in the spice mix. Leave to marinate in the fridge for a couple of hours, or preferably overnight. Remove from the fridge 20 minutes or so before you plan to cook so the chicken is not too cold.

Meanwhile, make the raita. Combine all the ingredients in a small bowl and stir together well.

Spear the chicken pieces onto bamboo skewers – about 3-4 chunks per skewer. Heat a little oil in a large non-stick frying pan (skillet) over medium heat and add the skewers once it's hot. Cook for 6-7 minutes, turning several times during cooking to make sure they get cooked and browned on all sides. Check that the chicken is cooked and opaque throughout.

Serve the skewers as they are with the raita for dipping, or remove from the skewers and pile the chunks into flatbreads, drizzling with the raita.

Dad's Malaysian Curry Bites

It's been a running joke in our family for years that our dad makes a great Malaysian curry; he always spoke about it but never made it so eventually our 'Dad's curry' ended up being created by our mum. We've adapted it here to create Malaysian curry bites to share or take on the go. We have also made them slightly healthier by using turkey mince, which is a bit less fatty than pork or beef and also high in feel-good proteins.

Serves 4 (makes about 16)

400g/14oz turkey thigh mince
1 large (US extra-large) egg, lightly beaten
2 tsp sea salt flakes
2 tbsp rice flour
groundnut oil, for shallow-frying
Little Gem lettuce leaves, to serve
kecap manis (sweet soy sauce), to serve

FOR THE SPICE PASTE
2 garlic cloves, roughly chopped
2 red chillies, roughly chopped (deseeded if you'd like them milder)
1 thick lemongrass stalk, sliced
2.5-cm/1-in piece root ginger, peeled and roughly chopped
2 shallots, roughly chopped

1 tsp ground turmeric
3 tbsp groundnut oil

Start by making the spice paste. Put all the ingredients in a food processor and blitz to a rough paste. Put the paste into a frying pan (skillet) and cook gently for about 5 minutes until it is smelling aromatic, then leave to cool a little.

Put the turkey mince in a large mixing bowl with the egg, salt and rice flour, and stir together. Add the spice paste and stir in until everything is well incorporated. Divide the mixture roughly into 16 and form each portion into a small patty.

Heat a little groundnut oil in a non-stick frying pan, so it just coats the bottom of the pan. Fry half of the bites at a time, for about 2–3 minutes on each side, until golden and cooked through. Remove from the pan and drain on paper towels.

Serve the bites with the lettuce leaves and sauce and let people assemble their own snacks: pop a turkey bite on a lettuce leaf, top with a little sauce, roll up the leaf and eat.

Mediterranean Veg and Halloumi Skewers with Bright Basil Oil

These skewers are really simple to make but super-healthy and delicious. Cook them under the grill, or on a barbecue as a great vegetarian option for friends and family. The bright green and amazingly fragrant basil oil is lovely to drizzle over and is also delicious drizzled over the Gluten-free Mini Pizzas (see page 110).

Serves 4 (Makes 8)

5 tbsp olive oil
2 garlic cloves, crushed
1½ tsp dried oregano
250-g/9-oz block halloumi, cut into 16 even cubes
8 cherry tomatoes
1 small aubergine (eggplant), or ½ a large one, cut into 2-cm/¾-in chunks
1 large red (bell) pepper, cut into 16 even chunks
1 small courgette (zucchini), cut into 2-cm/¾-in chunks
1 small red onion, cut into 8 slim wedges
sea salt and freshly ground black pepper

FOR THE BASIL OIL
25g/1 oz basil, leaves only
100ml/3½fl oz/⅓ cup extra-virgin olive oil
a pinch of salt

Before you begin, if you are using bamboo skewers, soak them in water for a couple of hours, which will prevent them burning under the heat.

In a small bowl, combine the olive oil, garlic, oregano and a good grinding of salt and pepper. Stir well.

Put the halloumi and all the vegetables into a bowl, and drizzle over the garlicky oil. Turn them gently in the oil (you don't want the onion or cheese to fall apart), then leave them to marinate for a couple of hours (or overnight, if you wish).

Meanwhile, make the basil oil. Put the basil leaves, oil and salt in a blender and blitz until the basil is broken down and the oil is green. You can pass it through a muslin (cheesecloth) if you like, for a finer result, or just leave it rustic like this. Set aside.

Thread the marinated vegetables and cheese onto the skewers, dividing all the bits equally. Brush a little of the oil that will have collected at the bottom of the bowl over the skewers.

Heat the grill (broiler) to hot and lay the skewers on a baking sheet. Grill (broil) for 10–15 minutes (keep an eye on them as grills differ a lot in their strength), turning occasionally, until the vegetables are softened and charred and the cheese is golden and beginning to melt a little.

Serve the skewers drizzled with the basil oil.

Blackened Tuna Bites with Creole Ketchup

These are on the spicy side of hot, but served alongside the chilled ketchup they are a taste sensation! The ketchup is really fresh and light, which complements the heat from the tuna.

Serves 6

500g/18oz tuna steak, cut into 2.5-cm/1-in cubes

FOR THE MARINADE
1 tbsp ground cayenne pepper
1 tbsp dried oregano
1 tsp salt flakes
2 tbsp olive oil
½ tsp freshly ground black pepper

FOR THE CREOLE KETCHUP
½ onion, roughly chopped
1 small celery stick, roughly chopped
2 garlic cloves, roughly chopped
1 red (bell) pepper, roughly chopped
2 tbsp olive oil
150g/5½oz fresh tomatoes, roughly chopped
1 tbsp chopped fresh oregano
sea salt and freshly ground black pepper

Combine all the ingredients for the marinade and add the tuna chunks. Mix gently until all the tuna is coated, then cover with clingfilm (plastic wrap) and pop in the fridge to marinate for at least 2 hours, or preferably longer.

While the tuna marinates, make the Creole ketchup. Put the onion, celery, garlic and pepper in a saucepan with the oil and sauté over gentle heat for a good 10 minutes until all the vegetables are soft. Add the tomatoes and oregano, and cook for a few minutes longer until the tomatoes have broken down.

Remove the pan from the heat and, using a liquidiser or stick blender, blend to a smooth sauce. Season really well with salt and pepper, and allow to cool. Once cool, pop it in the fridge to chill before serving.

Once the tuna has marinated, heat a non-stick griddle pan over very high heat. Put the tuna cubes in the pan and sear them for about 3 minutes, turning regularly so they get browned on all sides. (You may need to do this in batches, depending on the size of your pan – don't overcrowd the pan, or they won't brown properly.) Remove one from the pan and check that it has dark griddle marks on the outside, but is still pink in the middle.

Spear the tuna chunks on very small skewers or cocktail sticks (toothpicks) so they can be easily picked up, and serve with the chilled ketchup.

Dark Chocolate Chilli Tortillas

This is a lovely rich, deeply flavoured chilli, which is better made in advance as it tastes better the next day once the flavours have had a chance to blend and develop. You may have some leftover chilli, so pop it in the freezer for a handy quick meal another time.

Serves 6–8

1 tbsp olive oil
1 large onion, finely diced
2 garlic cloves, finely chopped
1 large red (bell) pepper, deseeded
   and roughly diced
400g/14oz beef mince
2 x 400-g/14-oz cans chopped
   tomatoes
1 beef jelly stock pot (bouillon)
1 tsp ground cumin
1 tsp ground cinnamon
1 tbsp sweet smoked paprika
1 tbsp smoked chilli paste (more if you
   like it hotter)
3 tbsp unsweetened cocoa powder
1 tbsp tomato purée (paste)
400-g/14-oz can red kidney beans,
   drained
about 2 tsp dark brown or molasses
   sugar
sea salt and freshly ground black
   pepper

TO SERVE
corn tortillas
sour cream
sliced red (bell) peppers
fresh coriander (cilantro) leaves
grated cheese
shredded Little Gem lettuce
lime wedges, for squeezing

Heat the oil in a large saucepan and soften the onion for about 5 minutes over medium heat. Add the garlic and pepper, and cook for another 5 minutes.

Add the mince and brown for a few minutes, then tip in the canned tomatoes. Fill each empty can about one-third full with water and swill it around to pick up all the tomato in the can, then tip it into the saucepan. Pop in the jelly stock and add all the spices, chilli paste and cocoa powder. Season and stir everything together well.

Let the chilli bubble away over low heat for about 40 minutes, until reduced and thickened. Stir in the tomato purée and beans, then taste and adjust the sweetness with a little dark brown sugar. Check the seasoning just before serving with the host of Mexican accompaniments.

SHARE THE LOVE

Spanish Serrano Ham Croquettas

These croquettas are absolutely delicious, especially when served hot, with their melting centres! They go very well with the smokey Paprika Ketchup on page 64.

Serves 4–6 (makes 12)

50g/1¾oz/3½ tbsp butter
60g/2¼oz/7 tbsp plain (all-purpose) or gluten-free flour, plus extra for dusting
500ml/17fl oz/2 cups whole (full-fat) milk
80g/2¾oz Serrano ham, in one thick slice, the finely diced
a grating of fresh nutmeg
2 eggs, beaten
50g/1¾oz/generous 1 cup panko or gluten-free breadcrumbs
vegetable oil, for frying
sea salt and freshly ground black pepper

Melt the butter in a saucepan over low–medium heat, then add the flour. Cook for a couple of minutes, stirring frequently, until the mixture is bubbling. Add the milk, a little at a time, whisking well between each addition.

Keep cooking for about 5 minutes, stirring continuously, until the sauce has thickened, then stir in the Serrano ham and season well with a good grating of nutmeg and salt and pepper. Transfer the sauce to a small shallow dish and cover with clingfilm (plastic wrap) so that the film is touching the top of the sauce (this will stop it forming a skin). Allow to cool a little, then pop it in the fridge to chill for an hour or so (or longer – you can do this the day before, if you like).

Once the white sauce is chilled, fill a saucepan about one-third full with vegetable oil and heat it over medium heat. It's ready when a few breadcrumbs thrown in start to bubble.

Put the dusting flour in one shallow bowl, the beaten egg in another and the breadcrumbs in a third.

Scoop ping pong ball-sized balls of the mixture (it should be quite set and almost jelly-like now) and roll it into 12 balls. Coat them first in the flour, then in the egg, then in the breadcrumbs. Once they are all coated, double coat them in the egg and breadcrumbs.

Fry the balls, a few at a time, for about 3 minutes, until golden and crisp on the outside and melted inside. Drain on paper towels before serving hot.

Slow-Cooked Soy and Honey Pork Belly Cubes

A great party snack that will get your friends' mouths watering.

Makes about 16

700-g/25-oz thick piece of pork belly, bones removed but kept, and skin scored (ask your butcher to do this for you)
150ml/5fl oz/⅔ cup dark soy sauce
3 star anise
peel and juice of 1 orange
3 tbsp runny honey
sea salt and freshly ground black pepper

Preheat the oven to 140°C/275°F/Gas Mark 1. Season the pork belly really well and set aside.

In a large, deep, heavy roasting pan, combine the soy sauce, star anise and orange peel with 250ml/8½fl oz/ 1 cup water. Stir well. Place the pork belly into the roasting pan, resting it on top of the bones that have been removed. Cover tightly with foil and put in the preheated oven.

Cook the pork for 3 hours, until meltingly tender and the cooking liquor has reduced to a syrup. Check the pork occasionally, especially towards the end of cooking, and if the liquid looks like it may start to burn, add a splash of water.

Once the pork has cooked (you can turn the oven off now), and cooled enough to handle, remove it from the pan and place it on a chopping board. Remove the skin and discard (or you can use this to make crackling), and place something very heavy on top; just make sure it's stable. Leave the pork to press while it cools down and is totally cold. Let the reduced cooking liquid cool in the pan.

Once everything is cool reheat the oven to 190°C/375°F/Gas Mark 5.

Skim as much fat as you can out of the pan and discard – you should be left with the reduced soy and aromatics. Pop the pan back in the oven for a few minutes to loosen everything, then add the orange juice and honey to the pan and mix well to make a glaze. If dry, add a splash more soy sauce.

Slice the pork belly slab into cubes about 3cm/1¼in square. Put them back in the roasting pan and baste with the marinade. Return to the oven for about 15 minutes, basting and turning halfway through, until the glaze is sticky and golden. Serve immediately.

Sausage and Mash-Up

A remix of hot dogs with the classic sausage and mash – we love this mash-up with ketchup and mustard on the side. Don't use new potatoes for this – you want floury baking ones, just small.

Makes 18

18 small white potatoes (about
   60g/2¼oz each)
18 good-quality gluten-free cocktail
   sausages
2 tbsp maple syrup
1 tbsp wholegrain mustard
2 tbsp olive oil
2 onions, sliced
1 tsp soft brown sugar
1 tsp balsamic vinegar
sea salt and freshly ground black
   pepper
American-style yellow mustard (such
   as French's), to serve (optional)

Preheat the oven to 190°C/375°F/Gas Mark 5.

Pop the potatoes on a baking sheet and bake for about 45 minutes in the lower half of the oven, or until golden and crisp on the outside and soft throughout.

Meanwhile, put the sausages in a bowl and add the maple syrup and wholegrain mustard. Mix well until the sausages are completely coated. Spread them out on a second baking sheet and, about 25 minutes before the potatoes are due to be finished cooking, pop them in the oven above the potatoes.

While the sausages and potatoes cook, heat the oil in a large saucepan over low–medium heat with a good pinch of salt. Add the onions and sugar, and cook them for about 20 minutes, stirring frequently, until they are caramelized and turning golden. Add the balsamic and cook until reduced right down and the onions are sweet and sticky. Check the seasoning and add pepper and more salt, if needed.

Once the potatoes are tender and the sausages are golden brown and cooked through, remove from the oven and slice the potatoes in half lengthways. Spoon about a teaspoonful of the onion mixture into each potato and top with a sausage and a squeeze of yellow mustard, if wished.

Spiced Lamb Samosas

What really makes the flavour of these samosas sing is the ajowan seed, which has an amazing thymey flavour. You can get it online or in specialist spice shops. But even if you can't find it, try these anyway without; they will still taste delicious and they are easier to assemble than you might think.

Makes 12

40g/1½oz/3 tbsp butter, melted
1 tbsp rapeseed oil
1 small onion, finely diced
1 large garlic clove, finely chopped
1 tsp ajowan seeds
½ tsp cumin seeds
½ tsp fennel seeds
½ tsp mustard seeds
¼ tsp ground turmeric
½ tsp ground coriander
1 tsp sea salt flakes
½ tsp coarse ground black pepper
350g/12oz minced lamb
6 large filo (phyllo) sheets

Preheat the oven to 180°C/350°F/Gas Mark 4 and grease a large baking sheet by brushing with a little of the melted butter.

Heat the oil in a frying pan (skillet) over low–medium heat and add the onion. Cook, stirring regularly, for about 5–6 minutes until they are softening and turning translucent. Add the garlic and cook for another 3 minutes.

Meanwhile, put all of the spices and the salt and pepper in a pestle and mortar and grind it all together. Tip the spices into the pan and cook for another couple of minutes until it's all smelling aromatic.

Tip the onion and spice mix into a mixing bowl with the lamb, and mix well to combine. Divide the mixture roughly into 12 portions.

Cut the filo sheets into strips about 10cm/4in wide and 35cm/14in long. Put them under a piece of clingfilm (plastic wrap), so that they don't dry out and become brittle, or they will become very delicate and difficult to roll.

Place a filo sheet on a work surface and put a portion of the lamb mixture into the bottom left-hand corner. Shape it into a rough triangle, following the edges of the pastry sheet. Flip the bottom left corner over, meat and all, so that what was the bottom short edge of the strip is now in line with the right-hand side of the strip. Flip the triangle over on itself again, in line with the pastry strip. Keep going for about 6 turns and the triangular samosa will have completely sealed edges, so that no meat can escape. Cut off any excess pastry, if there is any poking out from underneath. Repeat to make 12 samosas.

Place the samosas on the prepared baking sheet and brush liberally with the remaining melted butter. Put the sheet in the preheated oven and bake for 25–30 minutes until the pastry is golden and crisp and the meat filling is cooked through.

Gluten-free Mini Pizzas

Pizza has always been a favourite of ours, so we had to create a gluten-free version! Personalise your pizza with all of your favourite toppings.

Makes 8

275g/9½oz/2 cups gluten-free plain (all-purpose) flour, plus extra for dusting
1 tsp xanthan gum
7-g/¼-oz packet active dried yeast
1 tsp fine salt
2 tbsp olive oil
170ml/6fl oz/¾ cup warm water

FOR THE SAUCE
2 tsp olive oil
1 small garlic clove, crushed
200ml/7fl oz/generous ¾ cup passata
1 tsp dried Italian herbs
sea salt and freshly ground black pepper

FOR TOPPING
toppings of your choice, such as:
olives (green or black)
anchovies
slices of chorizo, salami or ham
sliced red onion
sliced red (bell) peppers
sliced mushrooms
mozzarella cheese, torn into pieces
fresh basil leaves, to serve (or even a drizzle of Basil Oil – see page 96)

Sift the flour and xanthan gum into a large mixing bowl and sprinkle in the yeast and salt. Pour in the warm water and olive oil, and mix everything together well until it begins to clump together into a dough. Tip the dough out onto a lightly floured surface and knead lightly until the dough is smooth. Wash out the bowl and grease it with a little more olive oil, then return the dough to it. Cover the bowl with a damp kitchen towel and leave it somewhere warm to rise for an hour or so. It won't rise as much as standard wheat bread, but should puff up a bit.

Meanwhile, make the sauce. In a small saucepan set over medium heat, cook the garlic in the oil for 30 seconds or so to cook out the raw flavour. Add the passata and dried herbs, and stir together. Cook for about 15–20 minutes, stirring frequently, until the passata has reduced to make a thick, rich sauce. Season well and set aside.

Preheat the oven to 220°C/245°F/Gas Mark 7 and put 2 large, heavy baking sheets in the oven to heat up.

Divide the pizza dough into 8 pieces and roll them out into small circles, about 3mm/⅛in thick. Smear the top of each pizza with a good spoonful of the tomato sauce, then top with whichever toppings you like, finishing with the mozzarella cheese.

Put 4 pizzas on each hot baking sheet and bake for 10–12 minutes, until the bases are crispy and the cheese is melted and tuning golden.

Once cooked, grind a bit of black pepper over each one and top with fresh basil leaves. Serve immediately.

Cauli-Cheese Quesadilla

Cheesy, veggie and gooey, this snack has serious comfort factor! You can use wholemeal or gluten-free tortillas, whichever you prefer. Our favourite are gluten-free sweet potato tortillas!

Serves 2–4

125g/4½oz cauliflower, chopped into
   very small florets (but not as small as
   cauli rice!)
15g/1 tbsp butter
15g/½ oz/1¾ tbsp. gluten-free or plain
   (all-purpose) flour
150ml/5fl oz/⅔ cup milk
75g/2¾oz Camembert or Tallegio
   cheese, diced
a grating of nutmeg
2 gluten-free soft wraps
sea salt and freshly ground black
   pepper

Blanch the cauliflower in a pan of boiling salted water for 2 minutes, then drain in a colander and set aside to steam dry.

Melt the butter in a small saucepan over low-medium heat and add the flour. Cook gently for 1–2 minutes until it goes bubbly. Add the milk, a little at a time, whisking well to get rid of any lumps. Continue to cook for a few minutes, stirring all the time, until the sauce thickens and it no longer tastes floury, then turn off the heat. Stir in the cheese until it's melted, then add a grating of nutmeg and salt and pepper to taste – go easy with the salt as the cheese will already be quite salty.

Place a large non-stick frying pan (skillet) over medium heat and put one of the tortillas in. Spread the cauli-cheese mixture over it. Place the other tortilla on top and cook for a couple of minutes until the base of the quesadilla is browned and starting to crisp up.

Carefully turn the quesadilla over. The easiest way to do this is by placing a board on top of the pan and flipping the whole thing over, using oven gloves (mits), so that the cooked side is face-up on the board.

Return the pan to the heat and slide the quesadilla from the board back into it. Cook for a few more minutes until the bottom is lightly browned. Slide it out of the pan and back onto the board, then slice it into wedges to serve.

Vietnamese Summer Rolls with Coconut Rice

The rice in these rolls lends a lovely coconut flavour to the filling, and makes this fresh and light summer snack just a bit more satisfying.

Serves 4–6

200g/7oz/generous 1 cup white basmati rice
400-g/14-oz can coconut milk
12 rice pancakes
360g/12½oz cooked king prawns (jumbo shrimp)
1 large carrot, peeled and juilienned
½ cucumber, seedy core discarded and length julienned
a small bunch of spring onions (scallions), trimmed and julienned
2 small red chillies, finely sliced
1 Little Gem lettuce, shredded
a small bunch of Thai basil
a small bunch of fresh coriander (cilantro)
a small bunch of mint

FOR THE DIPPING SAUCE
1 garlic clove, crushed
2.5-cm/1-in piece root ginger, peeled and grated
1 red chilli, finely diced
2 tsp fish sauce
4 tbsp lime juice
1 tbsp coconut palm sugar (or soft brown sugar)

Put the rice in a saucepan with the coconut milk and 100ml/3½fl oz/⅓ cup water and stir well until any lumps of coconut milk are broken down. Pop a lid on the pan and put it over low–medium heat. Once the liquid is boiling, set the timer for 10 minutes. Cook for 10 minutes with the lid on the pan, stirring a couple of times during cooking as the rice is more likely to stick and burn with the coconut milk in there. Once the 10-minute alarm goes off, move the pan off the heat and leave it to sit for 5 minutes, without lifting the lid, for the rice to finish cooking in the residual heat.

Meanwhile, combine all the ingredients for the dipping sauce and set aside.

Put the rice pancakes, prawns and all the vegetables and herbs on the table in separate bowls.

Once rested, spoon the rice into a shallow bowl and place on the table.

Allow people to dig in and build their own summer rolls, arranging a little bit of each ingredient in a line down the middle of a pancake. Tuck the edges in to seal in the fillings, then roll the pancakes up. Dip into the sauce and eat.

SWEET TOOTH

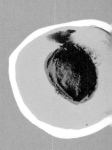

Banana Berry Sorbet

A bowl of this delicious sorbet contains two of your five-a-day, and the banana makes it really creamy. So easy to make, you just need a good blender.

Serves 2

2 bananas, cut into slices and frozen
160g/5½oz frozen mixed berries
4 tbsp freshly squeezed orange juice

Put the bananas and berries into a food processor and blitz until broken into small pieces. Trickle in the orange juice whilst blending, and keep blending until it forms a smooth mixture with the texture of soft ice cream. You may need to keep stopping the machine and scraping down the sides with a spatula to make sure it is all well incorporated.

Serve immediately, or store in the freezer until needed and allow to soften for 20 minutes or so at room temperature before serving.

Bitter Chocolate Ice Cream

Using low-fat crème fraîche in this ice cream gives it a lovely grown-up flavour, which works really well with the bitterness of the chocolate. It saves you making a custard, and cuts out a bit of fat and sugar, too. You can make this in an ice-cream machine, if you have one, adding the chopped chocolate towards the end.

Serves 6

600ml/20fl oz/2½ cups low-fat crème fraîche
4 tbsp unsweetened cocoa powder
3 tbsp maple syrup
100g/3½oz very dark (bittersweet) chocolate, chopped

Beat together the crème fraiche, cocoa powder and maple syrup until combined and you have an even colour, then stir in the dark chocolate pieces.

Transfer the mixture to a freezer-proof tub with a lid and freeze for an hour. After an hour, remove it from the freezer and beat it really well with a large spoon, being sure to pay extra attention to the edges of the tub where it will freeze more quickly.

Return the tub to the freezer and let it chill down again for an hour, then beat it again. Repeat about 5 times, until the ice cream is frozen to a soft set. Serve straight away, or keep in the freezer until required, removing it about 30 minutes before serving so that it can soften a little first.

Nutty Monkey Lollies

You'll need a set of six 50-ml/1¾-oz lolly moulds for this, which have a stand to keep them upright whilst freezing. The banana provides all the sugar you need, but if you'd like it sweeter, you could blend in a little maple syrup before you mix the peanut butter in.

Makes 6

2 large ripe bananas
100ml/3½fl oz/⅓ cup cream (dairy or
    soy)
a dash of maple syrup (optional)
40g/1½oz/⅙ cup no-added-sugar
    crunchy peanut butter, chilled so it's
    nice and firm

Place the bananas in the small bowl of a food processor and blend until smooth and frothy. Add the cream and blend it in. Taste; if you don't think it's sweet enough, add a little dash of maple syrup.

Add the peanut butter in small spoonfuls and pulse a couple of times to just start to combine – you want little pockets of peanut butter in the lollies so don't blend it in completely.

Tip the mixture into a jug (pitcher) and use this to pour the mixture into the lollipop moulds. Fill each halfway up, then go around again and top them up so that the final lollipop doesn't get all the peanut butter. Leave a little space at the top as they will expand when frozen.

Put the lollipops in the freezer for at least 4 hours, until frozen solid. To remove them from the moulds, dip the moulds briefly in warm water.

Watermelon Granita

Serve in small green bowls, sprinkled with black sesame seeds, for a real watermelon effect. This recipe doesn't take much work at all, but you do need to be at home all day to stir the mixture each hour, so it's a good treat for a quiet Sunday at home.

Makes as much as you like!

however much watermelon you have

With a sharp knife, slice however much watermelon you have and remove and discard the thick skin. Put the flesh in a food processor (in batches, if needed) and blitz until it is blended to a liquid. Pass the watermelon juice through a sieve (strainer), then tip into a freezer-proof container.

Pop in the freezer for an hour, then take out of the freezer and stir well with a fork to break up any ice crystals that are forming, particularly around the sides of the tub. Return it to the freezer for another hour and repeat. Keep doing this for a few hours and you will have a rubble of delicious watermelon-flavoured granita (you are looking for an appearance similar to very coarse sea salt). Pile into little glass bowls and serve immediately.

Retro Fruit Skewers

As 80s babies we love a bit of old-school party food. Cheese and fruit on a stick... simple but a real crowd pleaser. You can pop them in a box for a healthy snack on the go – and it's always more fun eating things off skewers.

Serves as many as you want!

a fruit of choice, cut into chunks
a cheese or choice, cut into large dice
a spice or herb to add a bit of extra
    flavour (optional)

Simply thread the fruit and cheese pieces alternately onto small bamboo skewers. Sprinkle with spice, herbs or other seasonings and enjoy.

Here are some ideas:

· Chunks of watermelon, cubes of feta and mint leaves.

· Pineapple and cheddar – but, of course!

· Stilton and fresh fig quarters with a sprinkle of cinnamon – to be a bit posh.

· Red Leicester, chunks of apple and a little sprinkle of dried thyme.

· Camembert and grape.

· Brie, apricot chunks and a drizzle of rosemary-infused oil.

Roasted Rhubarb and Ginger Swirl Frozen Yogurt

This is best enjoyed when rhubarb is in season. Using an ice-cream maker is best if you have one but if not then it's still possible, just make sure you pick a day when you're home as you will need to stir the mixture every hour.

Serves 6

600g/21oz rhubarb, chopped into
   3-cm/1¼-in lengths
1 tbsp pure vanilla extract
1 tbsp stevia granules
natural red food colouring (optional)
600g/21oz/scant 3 cups Greek-style
   yogurt
3–4 balls stem ginger, finely diced, plus
   2 tbsp syrup from the jar

Preheat the oven to 180°C/350°F/Gas Mark 4 and tip the rhubarb chunks into a roasting pan. Pop them in the oven and roast for about 20 minutes until completely soft.

Transfer the roasted rhubarb to a small saucepan and pop a lid on. Cook for about 5 minutes until the rhubarb is cooked down to a purée, then add the vanilla extract and stevia, and stir until the stevia granules are dissolved. If the colour of the purée is bit brown, add a little food colouring, then set aside to cool completely.

Put the yogurt in a freezer-proof tub, and add the stem ginger and ginger syrup. Stir well and pop the lid on, then put in the freezer for about 2 hours.

Once the rhubarb mixture has cooled, transfer that to another tub and pop it in the freezer with the yogurt. Stir the mixtures well every hour or so to break up any large ice crystals as they form, so that the mixtures don't set into solid blocks. Keep doing this for about 5 hours until both mixtures have firmed up, but are still malleable, then blob the rhubarb mixture into the yogurt mixture and swirl together gently so that there are swirls of rhubarb purée throughout. (You can, of course, freeze both mixtures in an ice cream machine and swirl them together afterwards).

Freeze a little longer until you have a soft scoop mixture, then serve. Or keep in the freezer and leave out to soften for 20–30 minutes before serving.

Prosecco Berry Jellies

A lovely summery jelly for when berries are at their sweetest and you want a special treat!

Serves 4

200g/7oz frozen berries
4 gelatine sheets
about 400g/14oz mixed fresh berries
1–2 tbsp light agave syrup (optional)
400ml/13½fl oz/1¾ cups prosecco

Put the frozen berries in a small saucepan with a lid. Cook over low heat for about 10 minutes until they have completely broken down.

While the berries are cooking, soak the gelatine sheets in cold water. Find 4 small, pretty bowls and fill each one with mixed berries, leaving a few to decorate the tops.

Pass the cooked berry mixture through a fine-mesh sieve (strainer) and discard what is left in the sieve. Taste the berry juice and add agave syrup to taste if it is a bit sharp. Squeeze out the gelatine sheets and stir them into the berry mixture while it is still warm so that they melt completely.

Open the prosecco and measure it out into a measuring jug (cup). Add to the berry syrup and stir them together gently, then pour the jelly into the bowls, dividing it evenly between them.

Place the jellies in the fridge for at least 2 hours to allow them to set. Decorate the tops of the jelly bowls with the reserved fresh berries before serving.

Turkish Pistachio and Rose Dark Chocolate Truffles

Rose extract comes in hugely varying strengths, so when making your own chocolate truffles, add ½ tsp, then taste and add more if you need to. Some are really potent and you don't want these sweet treats to taste like perfume!

Makes 12

100g/3½oz pistachios
6 large medjool dates, roughly
   chopped
100g/3½oz dark (bittersweet)
   chocolate, at least 70% cocoa solids
a pinch of salt
½–1 tsp rose extract
dried rose petals, to decorate

Put the pistachios in a food processor and blitz to a rough crumb. Remove 40g/1½oz and set aside. Add the dates to the food processor and blitz until they are well combined and starting to turn into a rough paste.

Put 60g/2oz of the chocolate in a heatproof bowl and melt it over a pan of simmering water, stirring frequently and ensuring that the bottom of the bowl does not come into contact with the water. Add the chocolate to the nuts and dates in the processor and blitz well to combine. Add the salt and ½ tsp of the rose extract and pulse a couple of times to combine. Taste and, if it's not quite rosey enough for you, add a little more, and repeat until it's the right strength.

Scoop the mixture out of the food processor and into a bowl. Cover in clingfilm (plastic wrap) and place in the fridge for 20 minutes or so for the chocolate to cool and firm up.

Meanwhile, and using the same bowl as you melted the previous chocolate in to save on washing up, melt the remaining 40g/1½oz chocolate over the hot water.

Remove the bowl from the heat and leave it for 15–20 minutes to cool and thicken a little.

Line a baking sheet with non-stick baking paper or a silicone mat, and set aside.

Put the pistachio crumbs on a plate and crumble a few large pinches of the dried rose petals into them, so that the green crumbs are flecked with pretty pink flakes.

Once the truffle mixture has cooled, divide it into 12 portions and roll each into a small ball. Spear a ball on the end of a skewer and dip it halfway into the melted chocolate. Allow the excess to drip off over the bowl, then dip it into the pistachio and rose mixture so that the nuts and rose stick to the melted chocolate. Place the ball on the prepared baking sheet. Repeat to cover all of the truffle balls, then leave to set before enjoying.

Chocolate-dipped Strawberries with Basil Sugar

Basil and strawberry is a classic combo. We've used stevia instead of sugar and coated them in dark chocolate, to make a healthy but indulgent treat. If you like, you can pop them on lolly sticks for a bit of fun!

Serves 2

6 large basil leaves
2 tsp granulated stevia
50g/1¾oz dark (bittersweet) chocolate
200g/7oz strawberries, leaves and
    stalks left on

Put the basil leaves in a mortar with 1 tsp of the stevia. Pound with a pestle until the basil is completely ground to a paste with the stevia. Stir in the remaining stevia. Spread out on a plate and leave somewhere warm for a couple of hours to dry out a little – it doesn't need to be completely dry, just enough to make a coarse crumble when you rub it between your fingertips, which you will be able to sprinkle.

Meanwhile, melt the chocolate in a heatproof bowl set over a pan of simmering water, ensuring that the bottom of the bowl isn't touching the water. Once melted, remove from the heat and leave to cool and thicken a little. Line a baking sheet with non-stick baking paper.

Using the stalks, dip the strawberries in the melted chocolate until half-coated. Whilst the chocolate is still tacky, sprinkle a little of the basil sugar over each strawberry. Leave to set completely before serving.

Fruit 'n' Nut Lollipops

As a general rule, the higher the cocoa solids, the better the chocolate is for you, so go for 95% if you dare... And if you want to add a touch of sparkle, add a puff of edible glitter spray to these sweet treats!

Makes 12

100g/3½oz dark (bittersweet) chocolate, at least 70% cocoa solids
fruit, nuts and seeds of your choice

Put the chocolate in a heatproof bowl set over a pan of barely simmering water, making sure that the bottom of the bowl does not come into contact with the water. Melt the chocolate gently, stirring occasionally, then remove the bowl from the heat and leave to cool.

The trick with these is to really cool the chocolate right down. If you try to shape the lollipops while the chocolate is still hot, they will run everywhere and you will have very thin puddles that the toppings won't be able to stick to securely. Leave the chocolate for a good 20 minutes at least, until it is lukewarm and has thickened up.

Meanwhile, cover a board with a sheet of baking paper (a few dabs of chocolate under the paper will help to stick it to the board and stop it moving at crucial moments). Using a dessertspoon, spoon puddles of chocolate onto the paper and carefully spread them out into neat rounds. Place a lollipop stick into each puddle and turn it in the chocolate so that the top is fully coated and hidden in the chocolate.

Now go mad with your toppings! Sprinkle on whatever dried fruit, nuts and seeds you wish, then leave to cool and set in a cool place (not the fridge or they may 'bloom' and get an unattractive white sheen on the chocolate). Once cool, peel the lollipops off the paper and enjoy.

Chai Spiced Figgy Fudge

Fudge, that's not made with processed sugar, but just with the natural sweetness of the dried fruit – winner, right? You will have extra chai mix left over here, so keep it for the next time in a sealed jar, or mix it into hot milk or coffee for chai-spiced drinks, such as the Chai-spiced Latte on page 35.

Makes about 40

500g/18oz dried figs, stalks removed
    and roughly chopped
2 tbsp coconut oil, melted
2 tbsp almond butter
2 tbsp unsweetened cocoa powder
1 tsp powdered coffee
a pinch of salt

FOR THE CHAI SPICE BLEND
seeds from 10 cardamom pods
¼ tsp black peppercorns
1 tsp ground cinnamon
1½ tsp ground ginger
½ tsp ground allspice
½ tsp ground cloves

Start by making the chai spice blend. Put the cardamom pods and peppercorns in a mortar and grind to a powder with a pestle. Add the remaining ground spices and mix everything together well.

Grease a container that measures about 16cm/6¼in square (if it's a little bigger it doesn't matter as you're not baking it) – you could use a small baking sheet or even just a plastic container. Cut a strip of non-stick baking paper the width of the container and use it to line the bottom and two of the sides – this will give you handles to pull the fudge out of the container more easily.

Put the figs in a food processor and blitz to a coarse paste. Add all the other ingredients, along with 1 tbsp of the chai spice. Mix and blend again until everything is completely incorporated. Taste, and add a little more chai spice if you'd like a stronger flavour.

Press the mixture into the prepared container and press down so the top is even (a potato masher is useful for this!). Fold the excess strips of baking paper down over the fudge to cover the top and pop the tub in the fridge for a few hours or overnight to set.

Once set, turn the fudge out onto a chopping board and slice into small squares. Store in a container in the fridge for up to a week.

Stuffed Dates

The ideas given here are suggestions rather than set recipes to show you what can be done with the humble date. Perfect if you fancy something small and sweet after a meal.

Makes as many as you need it to!

Medjool dates – a couple each is
   probably enough as they are so
   sweet
choice of toppings from the ideas here,
   or make up your own!

WHIPPED CREAM CHEESE

This is a great base for flavourings. Whip it up with an electric hand whisk until fluffy, and stir in ground cinnamon or ginger, coffee powder or unsweetened cocoa powder.

NUT BUTTERS

As ever, nut butters make a great choice for filling and topping. Try the ones in this book or buy them ready-made.

WHOLE NUTS

Roast nuts for a few minutes in the oven and stuffed in whilst still warm.

MARZIPAN

Whip up your own homemade marzipan, substituting the sugar for a bit of granulated stevia. Just blitz it all up in the small bowl of a food processor and stuff it into the dates.

CREAMY CHEESES

Brie, Camembert and goat's cheese, make a great filling for dates, so are perfect after dinner as they combine the dessert and cheese course!

Peanut Butter and Popped Quinoa Cookies

With the lovely toasty flavour of popped quinoa and roasted nuts, these cookies are crisp on the outside and soft and chewy on the inside. Use good-quality organic peanut butter if you can.

Makes 12

150g/5½oz/⅔ cup natural unsweetened crunchy peanut butter
100g/3½oz coconut palm sugar
1 egg
30g/1oz popped quinoa

Preheat the oven to 180°C/350°F/Gas Mark 4 and line a large baking sheet with non-stick baking paper.

Combine the peanut butter, sugar and egg in a mixing bowl and beat well with a wooden spoon until completely combined. Add the popped quinoa and mix again until thoroughly combined into a firm dough.

Divide the mixture into 12, roughly piling mounds of the dough onto the baking sheet. Once they are all about the same size, press them down and tidy up the edges a bit to form patties about 1cm/½in thick and 6cm/2½in across.

Put the baking sheet in the preheated oven and bake for 8–10 minutes until golden and crisp on top. Allow to cool and firm up on the sheet a little before serving warm, or cool completely and store in an airtight container for a couple of days.

Squirrels' Carrot Cake

The cake we were always allowed when we were growing up was carrot cake because it's healthier, right?! You'll be pleasantly surprised to hear that this recipe actually is, as it's full of nutritious and delicious ingredients.

Serves 8–10

400g/14oz/3 cups gluten-free plain (all-purpose) flour
1 tsp baking powder
1 tsp bicarbonate of soda (baking soda)
1 tsp ground cinnamon
1 tsp ground ginger
150g/5½oz grated carrot
100g/3½oz/¾ cup sultanas (golden raisins)
100g/3½oz/⅔ cup walnuts or pecans, coarsely chopped, plus extra whole nuts for decorating
2 bananas, mashed
60ml/2fl oz/¼ cup melted coconut oil
2 eggs, beaten
2 tbsp maple syrup or honey
120ml/4fl oz/½ cup almond milk (or another milk of your choice)

FOR THE FROSTING
100g/3½oz/scant ½ cup cream cheese
75g/2¾oz/5 tbsp butter, softened
1 tbsp maple syrup or honey
1 tsp ground cinnamon, plus extra to dust

Preheat the oven to 180°C/350°F/Gas Mark 4 and grease a 20-cm/8-in round cake pan.

Combine the flour, baking powder, baking soda, spices, carrot, sultanas and nuts a bowl.

In another bowl, combine the bananas, coconut oil, eggs, maple syrup and almond milk. Fold this mixture into the dry ingredients until everything is really well combined.

Pour the batter into the prepared cake pan and bake in the preheated oven for 20–25 minutes or until golden. Leave to cool in the pan for 10–15 minutes, then turn out and leave to cool completely on a wire rack.

To make the frosting, beat together the cream cheese, butter, maple syrup and cinnamon with an electric hand whisk or fork until all the lumps are gone and it's light and fluffy. Spread the mixture over cooled cake and decorate with the extra whole nuts and a sprinkle of cinnamon.

Lavender Rice Flour Shortbread

The rice flour in these shortbreads makes them really light and crisp. Using honey instead of sugar makes them a little stickier than normal shortbread, so be sure to chill the dough enough to cut cleanly. You can leave out the lavender for plain vanilla shortbread if you prefer.

Makes 12

100g/3½oz/7 tbsp butter
100g/3½oz/6 tbsp honey
1 tsp pure vanilla extract
120g/4oz brown rice flour, plus extra for dusting
50g/1¾oz/½ cup cornflour (cornstarch)
heaped ½ tsp culinary lavender

In a stand mixer, or in a mixing bowl and using an electric hand whisk, beat together the butter, honey and vanilla until smooth. Add the flours and beat again until well combined, then beat in the lavender until the mixture is smooth. Transfer the mixture to a smaller bowl and pop it in the fridge for a couple of hours to chill and firm up.

Preheat the oven to 170°C/325°F/Gas Mark 3 and lightly grease a large baking sheet.

Tear off 2 large sheets of non-stick baking paper. Dust the first sheet well with flour and spread half of the chilled dough over it (putting the second half back in the fridge), then dust the dough with a little more flour and place the second sheet on top. Using a rolling pin, and working quickly before the dough warms up and becomes sticky, roll the dough out between the two sheets to about 3mm/⅛in thick. (If it becomes too sticky before you have time to do this, just pop the baking sheet in the freezer for a few minutes.)

Using a 7-cm/2¾-in cookie cutter, cut out 6 rounds from the dough and use a spatula or fish slice to transfer them to the prepared baking sheet. You can quickly reform the scraps and roll out again with plenty of flour if you can't get 6 out of the first batch. Repeat with the second lot of dough to make 12 dough rounds in total.

Place the baking sheet in the preheated oven and bake for 10–12 minutes, until the shortbreads are light golden in colour. Allow to cool completely on the hot baking sheet before serving.

Raspberry and White Chocolate Crispies

These crispie bars are a real treat!
Use puffed brown rice for wholegrain
goodness and the best organic white
chocolate you can find. Freeze-dried
raspberries are available in the home
baking section of many supermarkets.

Makes 12

200g/7oz organic white chocolate
100g/3½oz/4 cups brown puffed rice
10g/⅓oz freeze-dried raspberries

Line a 20-cm/8-in square brownie pan
with a sheet of baking paper.

Put the white chocolate in a heatproof
bowl set over a pan of hot water,
ensuring that the bottom of the bowl
does not come into contact with
the water. Heat very gently until the
chocolate is melted.

Put the puffed rice into a large mixing
bowl and pour over the melted
chocolate. Mix everything together really
well, so that all the rice puffs are well
coated. Tip in the raspberries and stir
them through, then tip the mixture into
the lined brownie pan.

Pop the pan in the fridge for an hour
or so to let the chocolate set. Use the
baking paper to help you lift the square
from the pan, then slice it twice in one
direction and three times in the other
to make 12 pieces, and serve.

Coconut and Lime Loaf Cakes

The flavour in these cakes comes from the coconut oil (don't use the mild cooking stuff for this – you want the full flavour) and the whipped coconut cream on top. With a burst of citrus from the zest and juice of the limes, they're tangy treats that you'll want to eat time and time again.

Makes 6

100g/3½oz coconut oil, melted
100g/3½oz coconut palm sugar
2 eggs
100g/3½oz/¾ cup gluten-free plain (all-purpose) flour
75g/2¾oz/¾ cup ground almonds
1½ tsp baking powder
zest and juice of 2 limes
400-g/14-oz can coconut milk, put in the fridge for 24 hours
1 tbsp granulated stevia
15g/½oz coconut flakes, toasted, to decorate

Preheat the oven to 170°C/325°F/Gas Mark 3 and place 6 mini loaf cases on a baking sheet.

Cream together the coconut oil and sugar in a stand mixer or with an electric hand whisk. Add the eggs, one at a time, and beat in, then beat in the flour, almonds and baking powder. Finally add the zest and juice from 1 of the limes and mix briefly to combine.

Spoon the mixture evenly between the loaf cases and bake for about 15 minutes, or until golden and risen and a skewer inserted into one of the cakes comes out clean. Leave to cool completely on the baking sheet.

Remove the can of coconut milk from the fridge and open gently, being careful not to shake the can about too much. Scoop the top solid layer of cream off the top and put into a mixing bowl (the coconut water underneath isn't needed for this recipe but can be added to smoothies – see pages 36–37). Add the stevia and the juice of the second lime to the coconut cream and whisk with an electric hand whisk until thickened and fluffy, then whisk in the remaining lime zest.

Spoon the frosting over the loaves and decorate with a sprinkling of toasted coconut flakes.

Oaty Peach Melba Crumbles

A summery take on a traditional crumble. Full of flavour with no refined sugar needed, this peach melba-inspired crumble is the perfect way to treat yourself when peaches are at their sweetest in season.

Makes 4–6

200g/7oz raspberries
410-g/14-oz can peach slices in fruit juice, drained (or fresh if in season)
120g/4oz/1¼ cups whole jumbo rolled (old-fashioned) oats
4 tbsp mixed seeds
50g/1¾oz coconut oil, melted
3 tbsp maple syrup

Preheat the oven to 180°C/350°F/Gas Mark 4.

Divide the raspberries between 6 small (125-ml/4-fl oz) ramekins, or 4 slightly larger ones. Top the raspberries with the peach slices, halving any that are particularly big. The peaches make a good flat base to sprinkle the crumble over and stops it falling into the fruit juice and going soggy.

In a bowl, mix the oats, seeds, melted coconut oil and maple syrup. Divide the crumble mixture between the ramekins and place them on a baking sheet to make it easier to get them in and out of the oven.

Put the crumbles in the oven to bake for 25–30 minutes, until the crumble is golden and crisp on top and the fruit is bubbling hot.

Sticky Fig Brioche Tarts

These little tarts are really pretty and so easy to make. They taste indulgent and are made without loads of saturated fat or processed sugar. Using baked brioche instead of pastry cuts down on the fat making it a much lighter treat.

Makes 12

3 tbsp Marsala
1 tbsp maple syrup
1 sliced brioche loaf (you need 12 slices)
150g/5½oz/1½ cups ground almonds
2 small eggs
1 tbsp xylitol
¼ tsp baking powder
1 tsp good-quality orange extract
6 figs

Preheat the oven to 180°C/350°F/Gas Mark 4.

Put the Marsala and the maple syrup in a small saucepan and cook over gentle heat for a good 5 minutes, until the liquid has reduced to a glaze.

Meanwhile, roll out a slice of brioche with a rolling pin to flatten it. Cut the centre out with an 8-cm/3¼-in round cookie cutter and press the circle into a cup of a 12-hole shallow bun pan. Repeat to fill the bun pan.

Combine the almonds, eggs, xylitol, baking powder and orange extract in a mixing bowl, and beat until well mixed. Blob a small spoonful into the middle of each circle and spread out a little, but leave a clean border around the top edge.

Slice each of the figs into 8 thin slices and arrange 4 slices on top of each tart in a star shape. Using a pastry brush, brush a little of the glaze over the figs. (Keep the remaining glaze to one side.)

Pop the tartlets in the oven and bake for about 15 minutes, until the frangipane centre is puffing up and the figs are softened and becoming jammy. Brush the figs again with the glaze to make them shine, and serve.

Caramelized Grapefruit with Pineapple and Rum Syrup

A drop of rum makes everything fun! The syrup for this treat is made entirely from pineapple juice, so there's no added sugar. You need quite a powerful grill, or a chef's blowtorch to finish it off. You probably won't need all of the coconut cream, so pop the leftovers in the fridge and use it for the other recipes in this book, such as the waffles on page 28.

Serves 2

400-g/14-oz can coconut milk, put in the fridge overnight
200ml/7fl oz/generous ¾ cup pineapple juice
1 tsp rum
1 pink grapefruit, sliced in half

Start by making the coconut cream. Take the can of coconut milk out of the fridge and scoop the set cream off the top. Put it into a mixing bowl and beat with an electric hand whisk until light and fluffy. Pop it in the fridge until ready to serve.

Put the pineapple juice in a small saucepan and cook down gently for 5–10 minutes, or until the liquid has reduced to about 50ml/1⅔fl oz/3½ tbsp, and is thick and sticky. Stir in the rum and turn the heat off.

Preheat the grill (broiler) to high and line a baking sheet with foil.

Put the grapefruit halves on the prepared baking sheet. (If you need to, cut a slice off the top and base of the fruit so the halves sit flat on the sheet.) Drizzle as much syrup into the grapefruit as it will take, and spread it out over the top of the grapefruit. Put the fruit under the hot grill and grill (broil) for 5–10 minutes (this will depend on the strength of your grill) until the top of the grapefruit is darkening and caramelizing. If you like, use a chef's blowtorch to finish it off.

Allow to cool for a couple of minutes, then serve, drizzled with the remaining rum syrup and topped with a spoonful of coconut cream.

Chocolate Orange Shake

Like a drinkable, alcoholic chocolate orange – need we say more than YUM!

Serves 2

100ml/3½fl oz/⅓ cup almond milk
50ml/1⅔fl oz/3½ tbsp. triple sec
1½ tbsp unsweetened cocoa powder
ice cubes

Put all the ingredients in a cocktail shaker and shake until cold. Strain into glasses and serve.

Macadamia White Russian

A naturally creamy cocktail with a bit of nutty goodness. You need a powerful blender for this but you will not need all the cream, which is difficult to blend in smaller quantities. Just pop the rest in the fridge so that it's ready for enjoying a second glass!

Serves 2

100g/3½oz/¾ cup macadamia nuts
50ml/12/3fl oz/3½ tbsp Tia Maria or
    Kahlua
25ml/1fl oz/2 tbsp vodka
ice cubes

Put the macadamia nuts in a blender with 300ml/10fl oz/1¼ cups water and blend for several minutes until as smooth as can be. Pass it through a very fine-mesh sieve (strainer) to remove any unblended nut grains.

Combine the coffee liqueur, vodka and 100ml/3½fl oz/⅓ cup of the macadamia cream in a cocktail shaker with ice. Shake until cold, then strain into glasses and serve.

Watermelon, Cucumber and Gin Cooler

A refreshing and summery cocktail that's delicious and hydrating (at the same time as making you tipsy)!

Serves 2

500g/1lb 2oz watermelon flesh
100ml/3½fl oz/⅓ cup gin
100g/3½ oz peeled cucumber
a small handful of mint leaves, plus
**   a couple of small sprigs to garnish,**
**   if wished**
ice cubes

Put the chunks of watermelon flesh in a blender and blitz to a liquid. Pass it through a fine sieve (strainer) and get rid of any lumps of flesh and seeds.

Pour the melon juice back into the blender and add the cucumber. Blend really well until the cucumber is completely broken down, then add the mint, and pulse a few times until the mint is broken down, but flecks are still visible in the mixture.

Fill 2 long glasses with ice and pour over the cocktail. Garnish with mint sprigs, if you like, and serve.

Suppliers

While all our recipes use ingredients that are readily available in supermarkets or online, you might consider shopping at some of these specialist health-food shops, where you will also find our bars.

Amazon
www.amazon.co.uk
www.amazon.com

As Nature Intended
www.asnatureintended.uk.com

Bayley & Sage
www.bayley-sage.co.uk

Boots
www.boots.com

Borough Market
www.boroughmarket.org.uk

Holland & Barrett
www.hollandandbarrett.com

Ocado
www.ocado.com

Planet Organic
www.planetorganic.com

Riverford Organic Farmers
www.riverford.co.uk

Sourced Market
www.sourcedmarket.com

Squirrel Sisters
www.squirrelsisters.com

Whole Foods Market
www.wholefoodsmarket.com

Index

Thank You!

We would like to thank our amazing mum and dad (Jean and Bob) for being the most supportive and encouraging parents. You have given us confidence, inspired us to pursue things we are passionate about and always been there to advise. You really are the biggest Squirrel Sisters fans and we couldn't have done this without you. You're the best!

A huge thank you to our squirrel designer Ian, who also happens to be Sophie's husband.

Thank you to our amazing friends and family for always supporting Squirrel Sisters and our crazy ideas.

And finally, thank you to the amazing team at Pavilion for believing in us and giving us this incredible opportunity. Becci Woods, for all of your advice and making such delicious food; Sarah Epton, Laura Russell, Liz and Max Haarala Hamilton, Charlie Phillips and everyone that was involved in bringing the book to life. To Stephanie Milner, who found us and approached us with the recipe book idea and made it happen... as cheesy as it is to say, you really have made a dream of ours come true.